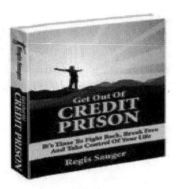

Over Twenty Years of Credit Experience

Author: Regis P Sauger

All materials contained here-in are the property of the R.Sauger Company under US Copyright TX0005895316/203-12-16 or otherwise referred to as being available under the US Freedom of Information Act.

ISBN: 978-1-68418-061-7

Original copyright registered in the US Library of Congress as document
#TX-5895-316 on December 16, 2003.
All rights reserved.
Published in the United States of America by Credit Educators of America
Gateway Blvd., Williamsburg Plaza, Suite 50 13 Orlando, FL 32821
Revised in August 2008 by Regis P Sauger
Edited and formatted by Christine Poremski

Written permission must be secured from the publisher to use or reproduce any
part of this book for any reason.
CREDIT PRISON
© 2003
NOTICE
The material contained in this book describes actual stories of real people. Names have
been changed at the request of those involved. The reference material contained in this
book is available to the public under the Freedom of Information Act.

This book was created as a reference, and describes strategies used by previous students.
While this book does contain legal information, it is not a substitute for qualified legal
advice.

The reader is advised to seek appropriate legal counsel before initiating any legal actions
discussed in this book.

ACKNOWLEDGMENTS

I give a hearty "atta girl!" and pat on the back to my staff for being "on
the go" from the very beginning of this project.

I would also like to thank:

Paul Barna	Timmy Pierce, Esq.
Will Bordelon	Roger Pope
Raymond Dunn	Ernesto Rolon
Ramon Faustmann	Dennis Villanueva
Bob Exton	Carolyn Roome
Houston Hill	Jess Lim
Axel Javier	Mike Reed Esq.
Angelino Llanardi	and others.
Pat Logue	
James McCord Jr	
James McCord Sr.	
Pearl Ocampo	

All materials contained here-in are the property of the R.Sauger Company under US Copyright TX0005895316/203-12-16 or otherwise referred to as being available under the US Freedom of Information Act.

1. About The Author 6

2. Money, Business And Greed 7
My First Understanding Of Money
My First Understanding Of Banks
My Introduction To Big Business
Greed And Golf Courses

3. Credit Past And Present...13
The History Of Credit
Bankruptcy Boom
Credit And Our Nation's Financial Security
Household Debt Is Soaring
Americans Are Over-Leveraged

4. Credit Reporting...16
Who Reports On My Credit? How
Is A FICO Score Calculated?
What Does A "Bad" FICO Score Mean?

5. The System – Why They Don't Want To Help You.............................18
Get Your Dates Straight
Mortgage Meltdown
The Mess On Wall Street And You
The Federal Reserve
Credit Card Companies
Collections Agencies
Why Would "The System" Want Me To Have Bad Credit?

6. The Law Is On Your Side.. 28
Fair Credit Reporting Act
Statute Of Limitations And Time-Barred Debts
Fair Debt Collections Practices Act
Truth In Lending Act

7. Dirty Tricks 33
Aging Your Account
Restarting Your Credit Prison Clock
Junk Debt Buyers

8. Dealing With Harassment.. . 35
Remember Your Rights
How To Stop Nasty Letters
How To Stop Nasty Phone Calls
When Was The Account First Late?

9. Negotiating With Creditors 41
Negotiate To Lower The Amount Owed
Negotiate To Re-Age Or "Cure" Your Account
Paying A Settled Amount

10. Small Claims Court... 46
Negotiating In Small Claims Court

11. Lawsuits And Judgments 48
Lawsuit Threats: They Must Read You Your Rights
Will They Really Turn My Account Over To An Attorney?
Statute Of Limitations
Getting Your Case Thrown Out Or Judgment Removed
Should You Go To Court?
A Credit Card Contract Is *Not* Proof Of Debt

12. Foreclosure 52
Home Equity Loans And Adjustable Rate Mortgages
Facing Foreclosure
Did You Refinance?
Defense Against Foreclosure
Stop Payments Now
Bankruptcy Is Not An Easy Answer
If You Are Being Sued
Beware Of Foreclosure Saviors!
The Bank May Not Own Your Home

13. Foreclosure - Refinancing And TILA Violations 57
Canceling Your Mortgage
TILA Audit
Rescission
Quiet Title
What Is The Difference Between Quiet Title And Rescission?
Look On The Bright Side

14. Auto Repossession 61
Was Your Car Sold In A "Commercially Responsible Manner?"
Was Your Car Damaged Or Stripped On The Way To Auction?

15. Medical Bills And HIPAA.. 65
How HIPAA Can Affect Your Medical Debts
How To Deal With Medical Collections

16. Cleaning Up Your Credit Report.. 67
A Quick Lesson in What Your Credit Report Contains
Get Copies Of Your Credit Reports
Review Your Reports For Errors

All materials contained here-in are the property of the R.Sauger Company under US Copyright TX0005895316/203-12-16 or otherwise referred to as being available under the US Freedom of Information Act.

Multiple Creditors For One Account
Multiple Account Numbers For One Account
Removing Same Name Information
Proving The Debt
Aging An Account
Time-Barred Accounts
Re-Aging Your Account
Rehabilitating Student Loans
Getting A Credit Reporting Agency To Correct Your Report
Injunctive Relief

17. Getting Started.. 78
Mental Preparation Make
Three Piles Organization
And Planning The Dispute
Process
Beware Of "Information Updated" Responses

18. Conclusion 83

Appendix: Statute Of Limitations By State..

All materials contained here-in are the property of the R.Sauger Company under US Copyright TX0005895316/203-12-16 or otherwise referred to as being available under the US Freedom of Information Act.

1. About The Author..................................

At one point in my life, I couldn't pay my bills, and went through a lot of the hassles you might be encountering now. In the process, I became fascinated with credit and how average people are affected by it. I was a man with a mission, and I have spent the last nine years researching the law, writing articles, and helping people just like you to escape from credit prison.

I am eighty-two years old, a retired PGA golf professional, a licensed Florida Mortgage Broker, author, national speaker, expert witness in US Bankruptcy, Oakland County and Michigan Circuit Courts, and I have advised insurance settlements relating to credit issues.

I do not hide any information from anyone, and I am dedicated to guiding you through the system, helping you raise your credit score, and eliminating the "grief" caused by scary bill collectors.

They call me "The Credit Professor", and my articles on consumer credit have been viewed by over 45,000 readers, and published in hundreds of newsletters nationally. I have conducted seminars for attorneys, bankers, underwriters, accountants, mortgage professionals, real estate professionals and the general public. Even my stepson, who is an attorney in Michigan, calls the "old man" occasionally for credit advice.

Today a lot of folks think that I am one of the top experts in the country on credit. I have appeared on the Larry King Internet Radio Show, Fox TV-4 News and WINK Radio and have been featured on websites all over the world. My articles have even been featured in an Oprah Winfrey show on credit. Am I smarter than anyone else? Nope, not at all. I am just dedicated to sharing knowledge, and I guess that being older and having white hair doesn't hurt.

The personal stories I share in this book are all true. I asked my attorney son if I would be exposed to libel or slander suits when I started writing this book. He said, "Dad, as long as you tell the truth, don't worry". So, the stories I share with you are either based on my personal experience, or have been the experiences of others, used with their permission.

This book is the culmination of my research and life experiences, and I think it's invaluable for deciphering foreclosure problems that have surfaced recently.

All materials contained here-in are the property of the R.Sauger Company under US Copyright TX0005895316/203-12-16 or otherwise referred to as being available under the US Freedom of Information Act.

The people that I talk about in this book are real live people with whom I have had a working relationship, and their names have been changed to protect confidentiality.

I created Credit Prison as a "learn at home" program, where you can do the research and work privately, and at your own pace. You can take your time, you can look for specific situations and you can even invite your brother-in-law over to help. (Unless he is like the typical brother-in-law who "knows it all," which results in nothing.)

Is it complicated? Well, if you have trouble understanding the inner workings of our system, keep reviewing this book – you will learn so much about credit that you could even turn out to be the family or neighborhood "*guru.*"

I encountered the tentacles of dealing with a convicted felon. I was duped, along with other prominent attorneys, accountants and business owners in believing this person posed as a Federal Fraud Examiner that worked for one of the major bank. If, I could be conned at my ripe old age along with other professionals, what chance did the public have. Un-raveling this mess was a nightmare and still continues today. If it almost impossible to delete derogatory information on the internet unless you have a "ton" of honest good stuff to offset it.

2. MONEY, BUSINESS AND GREED..

My First Understanding Of Money

As a society we are all users, lovers, benefactors, lenders, opportunists, and victims of money. Money affects our health, our ability to survive, and our self confidence. At some point we all become victims of greed, whether it is inflicted on us by others or it comes from our own personal desire to have more than we really need.

I think it's very important that the average person be able to relate to their own credit problems and eliminate the "guilt" that seems to be prevalent in our society. Our relationship with money begins when we are a little child, and continues to develop as we grow older. Here's a story of how I came to understand what a "dollar" is.

When I was a little boy, I knew that Daddy went to work and made lots of dollars. When he came home, he gave Mommy his paycheck and she gave me a dollar a week allowance. Sometimes I hid that dollar under my pillow for when I needed it. And when I went with Mommy to the store, sometimes I would bring some of my dollars to buy something. I knew that Mommy used the dollars that Daddy gets from his job to buy us clothes and things.

But where did Daddy's boss get all of those dollars? I asked, and Daddy told me that when he works, he made things. His boss sold those things and made some money. But Daddy said his boss also spends money, to pay for machines, materials, the factory, and a sales person to sell those things.

All materials contained here-in are the property of the R.Sauger Company under US Copyright TX0005895316/203-12-16 or otherwise referred to as being available under the US Freedom of Information Act.

I asked how the policeman and fireman get paid, if they don't make things? I think a part of daddy's check goes to pay them, it is called "taxes."

My First Understanding of Banks

Then I began to learn about banks. When my Dad's boss wanted to expand his business, he needed to borrow money. So a couple of local businessmen got together to form a new bank, which was run by Mr. Watson, who was a deacon at the church and showed up at everyone's wedding or funeral and smile.

The bank would take deposits of money from anyone, even my grandma or my piggy bank. They give me a little book and promised to pay me a small percentage in return for borrowing my money.

But it surprised me when I found out that they would take my money and loan it out to my neighbor so he could buy a car, and make money on my money. Was this fair? I guess so. It was called community banking. How did this work? They would pay my grandma 4% on her ten thousand dollar savings account for one year. So I got out my pencil and figured that at 4 percent of $10,000, my grandma would earn $400 in profit, and her money was safe in the local bank.

Meanwhile, the bank would take grandma's money and loan it out to farmer Johnson to buy a $10,000 tractor, which he promised to pay back with an additional 12% in interest, or $1,200.

I couldn't believe it! Mr. Watson was paying grandma $400 to use her money. And he was charging farmer Johnson $1,200.00 to use grandma's money. Without putting up any money of his own, Mr. Watson earned $800 and NEVER put up any money.

I checked my math again – that's right, Mr. Watson earned $800 and never had to put up any money – neither his own nor the bank's. Wow! I guess the community banks, world banks, governments and all the big shots already knew about how this worked too. No wonder everyone was so interested in the money business!

When I got to high school, my questions about dollars become harder to answer. I read the Magna Carta and Shakespeare's *Merchant of Venice* as class assignments, and I started to have new questions. As a teenager, I couldn't figure out why people made such a big effort to be elected to government. And then when I got to economics class I got really curious about European history – and started making connections between governments and money.

I wondered how the United Kingdom (England), a tiny country the size of Rhode Island, once controlled the shipping, trade, money, banking and armies of many other countries. How did they do this? And how did they allow America to win the War of Independence, which meant that we ended up controlling our own banks and armies?

All materials contained here-in are the property of the R.Sauger Company under US Copyright TX0005895316/203-12-16 or otherwise referred to as being available under the US Freedom of Information Act.

I just had to learn more about this amazing system. After I graduated from high school, I enrolled at the School of Hard Knocks and learned more about how the money system worked locally, nationally and internationally.

My Introduction to Big Business

In 1955 I joined the US Army. All five of my brothers were also were in the military, and my mother displayed each of her son's branch of service proudly in the front window of her home. Let me tell you, any flag burner or protester that came across my mom's path incurred the wrath of one proud woman! I have always been loyal to America, and I love my country. I just didn't know how much greed was in the system, or how it affected my fellow citizens.

After I was discharged from Fort Devens, Massachusetts I became a golf professional in the Boston area. I became friends with a man named Warren O'Donnell, who paid me a small commission when I played golf with him and his clients. I gladly took the money to feed my new family. Little did I know that this would be one of my first lessons about money, credit and greed.

Warren would find folks who wanted a loan but had credit issues, and invite them to a friendly round of golf. Between holes he would tell them that he could help them with their financing, but they would have to pay him a small percentage of what they got.

At the time, Tip O'Neil was a very influential person in Washington. He had taken the seat of John F. Kennedy in the House or Representatives, when JFK ran for the Senate. Tip was the Director of the Small Business Administration (SBA) prior to becoming a member of the House of Representatives in Washington. He maintained an office on the second floor of a building shared by two of his close friends: one was the president of a bank with offices on the first floor, and the other ran a branch of the Federal Government's Small Business Investment Corporation (SBIC) from an office in the basement.

This was a very cozy arrangement, as you will soon see. Here's how the deals went down. My friend Warren would meet a businessman who needed a loan at the Watertown bank and introduce him to the first player in the game, the bank president. The president would review his application, and say " I'm sorry, but your credit doesn't qualify you for a 6% bank loan. But if you go up the stairs to the SBA office, you might qualify for a government loan."

So Warren would walk the businessman upstairs to the second player in the game, Tip O'Neil. Tip would welcome him into his office and then say, "Gee, I'm so sorry that you weren't here last week to get one of our 7½% loans. We ran out of funds, and we don't get our next allotment of government money until next quarter. But if you really want your loan, I'll call Charley downstairs in the SBIC office and recommend that he gives you a loan today." Here we go, down the stairs to the third player. Charley would get him a cup of coffee, pull out some papers, have him sign and cut a check for exactly what he needed, minus points for Warren. The businessman would walk out of there with the new loan he needed – but he was now paying a rate of 9%.

All materials contained here-in are the property of the R.Sauger Company under US Copyright TX0005895316/203-12-16 or otherwise referred to as being available under the US Freedom of Information Act.

The trip up and down the stairs costs him 3%. Warren would get his commission and another deal was made in historic New England. Here is the story behind the scenes. I lived it and it is true. Warren's brother Kenny was a close aide to President John F. Kennedy. (How close? He was on the plane that flew the president's body home from Texas after he was assassinated.

Now you can see how powerful some of these folks are. When the Massachusetts Attorney General Edward Brooke put out the word that he was going to bring down this little deal (where the SBA was funneling people to high-interest loans to people like Warren) Bobby Kennedy, who at that time was the Attorney General for the US Government intervened. He pulled Edward aside and said, "Look, I found out that you have a personal IRS problem. Now, if you go away, your problem will go away". Edward resigned and his political career survived. (He was subsequently elected to the House of Representatives representing the people Massachusetts.

Edward was the last Republican Senator to be elected by this bastion of Democrats. Ironically, Barbara Walters recently disclosed in her upcoming memoir that she had an affair with Edward for several years in the 70's.) I am not going to include all of the stories that I wrote about in my other book, "The Other Side of The Coin". But I can't help but share one more of my favorites, which illustrates a lesson about banking greed.

Greed and Golf Courses

I was building the famous Boyne Alpine Course golf course in Northern Michigan for the pioneering developer Everett Kircher. While working there, I would end my day by having my glass of beer in the Snowflake Lounge before going home for dinner. One evening I could not help but overhear the conversation of a group of bankers who were at the resort for a convention.

Now at that time, if a bank had a state charter in Michigan, it could not own real estate. The thinking was that owning real estate put the bank in an unfair power position. Any bank that acquired real estate by foreclosure had to dispose of that real estate within a certain period of time. The only real estate the bank could legally own for a long period of time was the building that housed their offices.

I overheard the bankers in the Snowflake Lounge talking about an abandoned nine-hole golf course in Schoolcraft, Michigan. The First Federal Savings Bank of Kalamazoo had evicted the owner of the land and taken the property back. The story was that old Mr. Stiver, the property's owner, had given his son Gilbert the use of his farmland so that he could build the Olde Mill Golf Club. Gilbert ran into bad luck, and even though he managed to get the golf course open, the business failed. Apparently the golf course was abandoned and grown over with weeds.
A year later, after I had completed the course at Boyne, we were living in the thumb area of Michigan. We had two little kids and I needed a job. I told my wife one morning that I was going to Kalamazoo to buy a golf course. She said, "You're crazy -- we don't have any money!"

All materials contained here-in are the property of the R.Sauger Company under US Copyright TX0005895316/203-12-16 or otherwise referred to as being available under the US Freedom of Information Act.

I borrowed $20 from my mom and made the trip to Vicksburg, Michigan. I went to a branch office of the First Federal Savings Bank of Kalamazoo. I met with Mr. Edward Bauer and told him I wanted to buy the abandoned Olde Mill Golf Club.

He looked out of his front window and saw my red Cadillac convertible parked in front of his door, so he gave me an audience. He told me that the course was for sale for $275,000 and the bank required $50,000 down as a show of ability to purchase. I told him that I was going to give him $125,000 and *nothing down*. He looked at me as though I was a lunatic and was about to usher me out of his office. I said "Mr. Bauer, let me tell you why you are going to sell me that golf course this morning".

I told him that I already knew the bank was hiding the asset from the state examiners and that nobody was interested in the golf course or they would have at least cut the weeds down. They didn't even have a "for sale" sign on the property, to keep any bank examiners away. I told him that my down payment would be my ability to clean up the property. If I failed, at least the bank would have a current loan and an improved piece of property that they could now put up for sale and satisfy the laws of the state.

I walked out of there owning a golf course with no money down. This was one of my first lessons in street financing. Now that I owned a golf course, I still did not have any money. My first stop was to visit the Maple Lane Golf Club in Sterling Heights, Michigan, where I had started my career there as a caddy at the age of (10). The owner, who had a soft spot in his heart for me, provided the financial backing I needed to get any equipment I needed for my new venture. His son had a friend who was able to arrange a 90% SBA guarantee for a loan from any bank to build nine more holes. This is where it gets really good! It seems that when the bank in Kalamazoo evicted old Mr. Stiver, he was distraught because this was his family's farm and he was no longer able to live there. The bank moved him into town and he had a difficult time facing his former neighbors and friends because of what happened to him.

I befriended the old man and asked him to take a ride with me a couple of times a week to see what I was doing to the golf course and how it was cleaning up. One day, he said to me, *"Young man, I like you, because you are humble, honest and you respect me"*. He continued, *"Now, I want to tell you that the land that the 7th green and 8th tee sit on is **not owned by the bank**. The description in the abstract, which is a legal description of the land, did not include that piece. The bank has sold you a piece of land that they don't own. I own that land."*

I was shocked by what he told me next. He said, **"Young man, give me one dollar and I will give you a Quit Claim Deed to that piece of land."** (When someone sells you a piece of property for any amount of money, they can give you a Quit Claim Deed, which is a piece of paper that tells the world that they no longer have any interest in the property. This can be recorded in the county clerks office, but you can also just hold onto it until you really have to prove you own the property.) Mr. Stiver continued, "I am too old to fight and don't have the energy. But maybe you can use it to your advantage".

All materials contained here-in are the property of the R.Sauger Company under US Copyright TX0005895316/203-12-16 or otherwise referred to as being available under the US Freedom of Information Act.

Read on to find out how this really put the professor's degree in finance into play. It was time to go back to Ed Bauer at First Federal Savings Bank of Kalamazoo. I already owed his bank $125,000, and now told him I wanted to borrow an additional $200,000 to build nine more holes. He laughed at me until I told him about the 90% guarantee from the US Government. Ed Bauer took the deal to the board of directors and they approved it. Little did they know what surprises were still in store!

At the end of the deal, we were getting ready to sign the closing documents and I poked my partner and my attorney in the sides and said, "keep quiet." I then looked at Ed Bauer and the other bank officers and said, "I'm sorry, but we cannot close on this loan. You have sold us property that you don't own". I then told them about Mr. Stiver and how he owned the land on which a tee and a green sat. I said, "We have been damaged, because we have spent money and time to improve that portion of the golf course and you don't own it."

They went ballistic! The closing was postponed until the lawyers could have the title company check my claim that Mr. Stiver still owned of a portion of the land. The bank's top brass joined the meeting after lunch and didn't know what to say or do. After all, they had evicted and humiliated the old man, and knew that he would slam the door in their face if anyone from the bank approached him to buy that land.

I said, "Gentlemen, we all know the legal problems with this property. You want to charge us 7% on this loan. If I can get Mr. Stiver to sign a Quit Claim Deed, I want you to reduce the loan rate to 5%. Take it or leave it". The bank, knowing their very weak position, reluctantly agreed to the new terms, which would end up saving me over $65,000.

I pulled the Quit Claim paperwork from my jacket pocket and said, "The old man likes me because I have included him in our daily schedule. If you sign this loan commitment for 5% right now, the Quit Claim is yours. The bank president signed the loan commitment, and I signed the claim. You could not believe the looks on everyone's face when I pulled this off. The bottom line is that I am a child of the depression, and I know that greed makes people do strange things.

In my lifetime I have seen and experienced shameful political business decisions by both Democrats and Republicans. I have watched lawyers switch sides for a bigger payout. I have watched honest men who pay their bills on time get wiped out because of backroom deals cooked up by crooked bankers. I have seen many different flavors of fraud, scams and negligence. *I always get as much knowledge about a deal as I possibly can.*

When you buy a business, dig into its history: did the business incur any legal issues, such as fines? When you buy a piece of property, ask how old the plumbing, roof, electrical and other services are. Find out if the seller has personal financial or marital problems. You can find this information out simply by starting a conversation. You may be able make a big difference in the price and down payment, if you find out that the seller is hiding something from the government or his soon to be ex-wife. Knowledge is power, so learn to get it and use it without hurting anyone.

All materials contained here-in are the property of the R.Sauger Company under US Copyright TX0005895316/203-12-16 or otherwise referred to as being available under the US Freedom of Information Act.

3. CREDIT – PAST AND PRESENT ....

The History of Credit

Under the Freedom of Information Act, I found a fascinating published article called "Our Credit System's Debtor's Prison – Full Circle". The unknown author shows that in order to understand our present day credit system, we need to look back in history and learn that credit was utilized over 3,000 years ago.

Do you suppose it might be possible to have a sufficient number of consumers declare bankruptcy that the entire economy might implode upon itself? Though credit was first used in Assyria, Babylon and Egypt 3,000 years ago, an article at Newsweek MSNBC suggests that early civilizations had far higher interest rates and crueler punishments for failing to repay loans than we have today. It seems that in Athens, for example, enslaving debtors was common practice – but was eventually seen as impractical, as the farming class all fell into debtor's slavery. The outcome was no crops grown, and no one having anything left to eat.

Picture our country with all of the farmers either bankrupt, in prison or out of business. Who would feed the army? Could what happened thousands of years ago repeat itself? Just look at the effects of the "dust bowl" during the Great Depression, and how today's "family farms" are being lost to big corporate entities.

The Babylonians' Code of Hammurabi set rates at 33 percent but the Roman Emperor Constantine set a much lower rate at 12.5 percent. Then the Catholic Church went on a crusade against usury (meanwhile selling "forgiveness of sins" in the form of plenary indulgences to those with money to pay for it.) Regardless, the Magna Carta placed limits on interest in 1215.

The first advertisement for credit was placed in 1730 by Christopher Thornton, who offered furniture that could be paid off weekly. But In 1752, Britain tried to forbid the New England colonies from issuing bills of credit.

Ironically, colonists ended up financing the revolution with the same bills that Britain so despised along with a flood of hyper-inflationary paper money. But use of one form of credit continued. From the 18th to 20th century, "tallymen" sold clothes in return for small weekly payments. They were called "tallymen" because they kept a record or tally of what people had bought".

Remember Harry Bellafonte's lyrics, "Come Mr. Tallyman, tally me bananas?" According to Newsweek MSNBC, President Andrew Jackson crusaded against the United State's National Bank in the 1820s, seeing it as an elitist vehicle for corruption. After the Civil War, the whole country felt shaky about using paper money as legal tender, instead of notes backed by gold or silver. It took 30 years to settle on our current currency.

All materials contained here-in are the property of the R.Sauger Company under US Copyright TX0005895316/203-12-16 or otherwise referred to as being available under the US Freedom of Information Act.

The Federal Reserve is the successor to the very first US National Bank. Having access to "easy credit" is a primary cause of our country's current financial mess. Did you know that the Federal Reserve Bank implemented a policy of "easy credit" in the 1920s that prolonged the boom years – and also heightened the crash of 1929? Credit cards did not arrive on the scene until 1950, when the first Diner's Club charge card was issued to 200 friends for use at 14 restaurants in New York City. Diners Club was immediately followed by American Express in 1951. The magnetic strip was introduced in 1970, and ushered in the credit card industry boom that has driven our economy for decades.

The founder of Diner's Club had no idea that 45 years later more than 90 percent of all U.S. transactions would be made electronically. He just figured it would be an easy way to avoid embarrassment when he was short of cash for dinner.

Bankruptcy Boom

While we no longer have a debtor's prison, and "usury" is supposedly illegal, credit still drives our economy. The credit card has been the single major pivot in creating a boom in bankruptcies. *Do you suppose it might be possible to have enough consumers declare bankruptcy that the entire economy might implode upon itself?*

Thinking back to how the Babylonians starved when their farmers were all in debtors prison, I have to imagine that it's possible. You have to be careful when your castle is built on plastic.

Credit And Our Nation's Financial Security

How does credit affect our nation's financial security? Even our founding fathers knew we needed to be careful:

"**No generation has a right to contract debts** greater than can be paid off during the course of its own existence." – *George Washington to James Madison 1789*

"We hear sad complaints sometimes of merciless creditors; whilst the acts of **merciless debtors** are passed over in silence." -*William Frend, 1817*

"There is no means of avoiding **the final collapse** of a boom brought about by credit **(debt) expansion**. The alternative is only whether the crisis should come sooner as the result of a voluntary abandonment of further credit (debt) expansion, or later as a final and total catastrophe of the currency system involved."- *Economist Ludwig von Mises*

"Growing domestic and international debt has created the conditions for **global economic and financial crises**." – *Bank for International Settlements June 2005*

All materials contained here-in are the property of the R.Sauger Company under US Copyright TX0005895316/203-12-16 or otherwise referred to as being available under the US Freedom of Information Act.

Household Debt Is Soaring

Household debt is primarily made up of mortgage debt and credit (credit cards, auto loans, etc.). If household debt were not growing faster than the economy's meaning household debt is increasing faster than our economy is growing. Today's household debt ratio is 123%, which is triple the debt ratio of 1985. What does this mean? Well, it suggests that real equity has not the driving force of our nation's economic size. Our economy has been driven by debt. Our economy is more leveraged by household debt than ever before, and households are at the mercy of credit and mortgage interest rates more than they have ever been before.

Americans Are Over-Leveraged

Mortgages - In 2007, mortgage debt was $10.5 Trillion, or 76% of the $13.8 Trillion total household debt. It was estimated in March 2008 that only $587 billion (5.5%) of equity supports the mortgage total, meaning that on average, **mortgaged houses were leveraged 18 times**. Keep in mind that this ratio was quoted at a time housing prices were falling dramatically, meaning the supporting equity ratio is also further declining.

The equity in all homes nation-wide had fallen to the **lowest home equity ratio in history** even before prices recently started their dramatic plunge.

Auto Loans - According to USA Today (2/16/04), the *length of the average automobile loan today is for 63 months, with some going as high as 80 months*, compared with an average of less than 48 months five years ago - - and about 24 months in the 1950s. In 1997, banks financed an average of 89% of a new vehicle's price. Last year banks were financing 101% of a new vehicle's price, since consumers borrowed to cover the amount they were upside-down on their trade-in. And get this: 40% of all trade-ins now involve upside-down car loans! I remember that when I entered the workforce in the late 1950s, the normal down payment on a car was one-third cash, and 18 month financing for the balance. How times change!

Credit Cards - A massive **42% of Americans who have credit card are making just minimum payments – or no payments – on their credit card balances**, according to the Cambridge Consumer Credit Index in March 2004. Another 39% paid less than half the balance owed but more than the minimum. According to the research firm CardWeb.com, in 2003 the average credit card debt of US households with at least one card was $9,205, up from $2,966 in 1990 – an increase of 310%. The same firm said, "about 51 million households carry credit card debt at an average balance of nearly $12,000."

Families And The Younger Generation - How can such debt trends be sustained? The trends are even more alarming when you consider that real median incomes for families have been stagnant for 2½ decades, as income of full-time working males has fallen for more than a decade. (Grandfather Family Income Report) Despite the fact that families can expect much less in pension benefits when they retire than their elders, they are more likely to consume their home equity than prior generations. (Grandfather Social Security Report)

All materials contained here-in are the property of the R.Sauger Company under US Copyright TX0005895316/203-12-16 or otherwise referred to as being available under the US Freedom of Information Act.

The real price of college education continues to increase as tuitions rise and the quality of a high school education declines. (Grandfather Education Report) There have been tremendous increases in inflation-adjusted public spending per student, even while American students are testing more poorly than their international peers than ever before. The result of this waste of individual and national resources is that families and students take on more college debt than ever before. And when they graduate, these students will face global competition for their living standards more so than any generation in U.S. history.

America's energy infrastructure has deteriorated and depends heavily on other nations to provide petroleum and natural gas resources. *America used to be the biggest creditor – but as our trade deficits continue to explode, we are now the biggest international debtor in the world.* (Grandfather Foreign Trade Report.)

4.CREDIT REPORTING..

Who Reports On My Credit?

Consumer Reporting Agencies (CRAs) are organizations that collect and share information about consumers, to be used in credit evaluation and other purposes. The three CRAs – Equifax, Experian and TransUnion – are privately owned, and are in business for one reason: PROFIT. They are paid by the creditors who furnish your information to them – these creditors are their customers. You are not a customer to CRAs – you are nothing more than a product, and you don't even "own" your own credit report.
To repeat, creditors are the CRAs' only source of income. So ask yourself why in the world would they be motivated to you? The CRAs will always favor the creditor because they know where their bread is buttered. They want to keep the
cash flowing, plain and simple.

How Is a FICO Score Calculated?

Fair Isaac is the company responsible for the FICO credit scoring system used for years by lenders to rank one borrower against another, judging them for credit risk. The three Credit Bureaus use this Fair Isaac scoring system to calculate your FICO score based on the information

they have on your credit history. Because there are discrepancies in the information on file at each of these three agencies, and because they may apply the scoring system differently, you could discover that your FICO score at Equifax is different from TransUnion, which again could be different from your Experian score.

First, they place you into one of 10 credit categories according to your actual use of credit. People with lots of credit are compared to other people with lots of credit. People who have limited credit are compared to other people with limited credit, etc. – this sounds fair so far.

All materials contained here-in are the property of the R.Sauger Company under US Copyright TX0005895316/203-12-16 or otherwise referred to as being available under the US Freedom of Information Act.

They then assign you a neutral score — about 600 points, according to a Fair Isaac spokesman – and then add or subtract points according to "good" or "bad" use of credit.

Their scoring is impartial. They don't know who you are, and have no agenda other than to score your past credit habits and give lenders a snapshot of how your credit history will play into your intention and ability to repay future loans.

There are five measures that account for the bulk of your FICO score. **The first 35% of your score is based on past credit repayments.** You get points added for paying bills on time, and you get points subtracted for paying bills late. It's that simple: pay your bills on time and fully one-third of your FICO credit score will shine.

You also will have points subtracted for non-payments and restructured payments (negotiated payments where the lender takes less than originally agreed), as well as bankruptcies. The more severe the credit problem is, the more points are deducted. For example, you'll lose more points for a bankruptcy or a write-off than you will for being late with a credit card payment. **30% of your score is based on the ratio between how much you owe and the total available credit you currently have.** The lower the ratio, the higher the score. For instance, if you have a ratio of 25%, you will score higher than someone who has maxed-out credit cards, or little or no home equity.

15% of your score is based on your past management of credit, the actual length of time you've borrowed money and paid it back. Having "good" credit here isn't the issue -- long-term, proven credit usage is what is being measured. Someone with limited credit experience, maybe one or two years of using credit, will score lower here than someone who has a credit going back decades, even though there could have been some "bruised credit" somewhere along the way for the second borrower.

10% of your FICO score measures how many different types of credit you have handled successfully in the past.
If you've borrowed money to buy a home, buy a car, pay for a college education, and you have several credit cards that you pay religiously every month, your score will be higher than that person who has only applied for a car loan. Having a broader range of credit experience helps in this area.

10% of your FICO score depends on how many times potential lenders look at your credit file. This one is the most infuriating for me. I personally have had my credit report "dinged" for too many credit inquiries, especially when I explored refinancing options a few years back. Every mortgage broker I called to get home loan quotes pulled my credit report, and one even pulled it twice. These inquiries weren't supposed to affect my score, but I watched my actual score start to go lower.

All materials contained here-in are the property of the R.Sauger Company under US Copyright TX0005895316/203-12-16 or otherwise referred to as being available under the US Freedom of Information Act.

The inquiries made by you, your employer or an insurance company aren't supposed to affect your final FICO credit score, although they do show up. Credit report queries should only appear on your report when you apply for credit. However, it seems that having a large number of those inquiries in a short period of time will make this portion of your FICO score suffer. Why? According to the folks at Fair Isaac, people who apply for many lines of credit in a short period of time have been shown to be 800% more likely to file for bankruptcy.

What Does a "Bad" FICO Score Mean? Simply put, the lower your credit score, the higher the interest rate charged, and the harder it is to get a loan. People who have a low credit score have fewer options to negotiate for the lowest interest rates, and they often cannot qualify for low- or no-fee loans. The extra money spent over the life of the loan can be substantial. As an example, a person with a low FICO credit score will pay about $200 more every month on a $200,000 home loan than someone with great credit, according to Fair Isaac. The hypothetical borrower above would pay over $70,000 more over the life of his loan than the higher-credit borrower would. The difference --and importance of -- these examples underscore how important having a good credit score can be.

5. THE SYSTEM & WHY THEY DON'T WANT TO HELP.....

Lace up your boots, strap yourself in and listen up. This is the beginning of your quest to understand this credit course and learn how you got where you are and what you need to get where you want to be. At one time we all had excellent credit or at the least, decent credit. You probably had every intention of paying your bills. If you are one of those that want to beat the system, you are reading the wrong book, Charlie. But if you want to understand the system and learn how knowledge can raise your credit scores, you owe it to yourself to study this book.

It is a fact that over 85% of today's credit reports have some type of an error. Remember, data is entered by humans, who make mistakes. Here's a true story – I once saw a situation where a couple with excellent credit went car shopping in Texas on a Friday afternoon. On Monday another couple in Boston, with the same name and similar social security numbers, had an entry on their credit report that showed they had just bought a car in Texas. Because credit reports are so difficult to understand, it's very easy to just look the other way. It used to be that you only needed a good credit report when you were going to buy a house or a car. But these days, high credit card interest charges are becoming ridiculous to live with, and credit is important to everyone, all the time. So how do we attack this beast? With knowledge of the system.

Get Your Dates Straight In this book you will hear me talk a lot about Section 623(a)(5) of the Fair Credit Reporting Act. In this law, the US Congress mandated that derogatory credit must be removed from your credit files after 7 years. *The big question is: when does this 7-year period start?* By the time you finish this book, you will know Section 623(a)(5) by heart. It is the bible of the credit industry, and is a weapon to defend yourself from greedy collectors and unscrupulous lawyers who buy up what is called time-barred debt. (Read more about this in Chapter 6.) Think of this as is your private credit PIN number from me.

All materials contained here-in are the property of the R.Sauger Company under US Copyright TX0005895316/203-12-16 or otherwise referred to as being available under the US Freedom of Information Act.

Here is an example of why the date is so important. Let's say that Joe bought a refrigerator on credit from Honest Harry. A year later, Joe had a problem with the refrigerator, but Harry refused to fix it. Now we have a problem – Joe is mad at Harry and Harry refuses to talk to Joe. This goes on for over four years, and finally Honest Harry sells this old debt to a collection agency for pennies on the dollar.

Joe bought the refrigerator in January 2003 and quit paying on it in June of 2004. The law says that June 2004 is the actual date from which the (7) year period starts. Here is where Joe will get caught in a trap and not even know it. Let's say that Harry sold the account to Larry Leech in July 2008. Larry Leech reports on Joe's credit report that the refrigerator account was first late in July 2008, which is when he first got received Joe's delinquent account. Happens everyday.

So instead of the seven-year clock starting in July of 2004, it doesn't start until 2008. Having a delinquent item on your report is like being sentenced to credit prison – and Joe just had four years added to his sentence. In technical terms, Larry Leech just "aged" Joe's account, which is a violation of Federal Law and punishable by a fine of $1,000.

Remember, the Credit Reporting Agencies are paid by creditors, and creditors like to keep you in credit prison, so that you'll have to pay higher rates. They "age" accounts all the time, and very few people ever stop them.

Mortgage Meltdown

What caused the mortgage meltdown that we are witnessing today? Well get comfortable, because I'm going to describe the whole dirty scheme as I see it to you here – and my version of the story is confirmed every time a new villain is uncovered. A massive "scam" on the American public was hatched in the minds of greedy bankers starting back in 1983, when they created a monster called an **asset based trust**.

Let's say that you bought a home for $300,000, and that you got a mortgage from your friendly banker at an interest rate of (8%). That works out, to an annual interest payments that start at $24,000 and becoming smaller each year as the principal is paid down. Now these greedy financial geniuses decided to buy up thousands of mortgage notes and put them into one basket. They paid the mortgage companies (big or small) a commission, or "service release premium," of around 2% for selling these mortgage notes to them. In the process, your friendly banker down the street made $6,000 (2% of $300,000) on the sale without putting up a dime for your mortgage. What a business! Don't you wish that you could make that kind of money for just being a middle man?

Now the group of scam artists that put all of these zillions of dollars of purchased mortgage notes into a basket decide to re-name the basket as an "asset-based trust." Once they created this new trust, they have the ability to start playing with the numbers. *To cover their trail, the lenders instruct their attorneys to not find the note.* The yield they get for your note is $24,000.

All materials contained here-in are the property of the R.Sauger Company under US Copyright TX0005895316/203-12-16 or otherwise referred to as being available under the US Freedom of Information Act.

Originally, that yield was based on earning 8% on 300,000. But they could also earn the same yield by changing the rate to 6% on 400,000. So they took the liberty of changing the value of your loan from $300,000 to $400,000. This adjustment did not affect you, but increased the value of the overall trust, and thereby increased their commissions by 25%. **This transfer of your mortgage note to an asset-based trust was a fraud on the courts, and on the American public.**

Within this asset based trust were the instructions on how to manage the assets. This is called a "pooling and servicing agreement". Now, all of this is recorded and filed with the Securities and Exchange Commission making it all legal (we thought). Now, this pooling and services agreement mandated that the asset manager MUST replace non-performing paper with performing paper to insure the integrity of the trust and protect the investors.

READ CAREFULLY: Here is where their greed tripped them up. They thought that because a performing note at .06% could easily be replaced by a toxic or sub-prime loan that was earning .14% and it was 100% insured by AIG, they simply put the spread in their pockets. You figure it out on hundreds of thousands of mortgage notes. Lets say they average $200,000 @ .06% that would yield to the investor or the trust $12,000 per year. But, when they replaced that good loan with a bad loan that was earning .14% go ahead and figure it out. It amounts to the difference of .08% or a sneaky profit of $16,000 on one loan. These guys are the ones that should be in prison. But, the politicians still keep playing "footsie" and pointing fingers.

Fraud #1: When the new lender served you foreclosure papers on your house, they swore under the penalty of perjury that they indeed were the owners of the original note and had possession of the note. But then in another part of the lawsuit, they ask the court to accept a "lost note affidavit" because they cannot find the notes. I ask, how in the hell can you lose something you never owned in the first place?

Fraud #2: The new lender changed the terms of your loan without notifying you. By law, all parties must agree to any changes to the original agreement – or the agreement is no longer valid. So, here we have this financial mess, and every politician understands it. The Republicans and Democrats know that they must work together to bail out the bankers, or there will be chaos on Wall Street.

How deep does the mess go? As you know, there are a lot of shady people in this world who have piles and piles of cold cash. Who are they? Let your mind wander a little... if you are a narcotics dealer, an arms dealers, or a kidnapper, what good is your cash locked up in a room somewhere with armed guards looking on? Lo and behold, here comes a chance for you to purchase – for cash– an investment in this basket of American mortgage notes without revealing your name. That's correct! When you purchase an investment into this basket of notes, you are simply assigned a number and recorded as a "book entry." Your profit can easily be wired to the bank of your choice, perhaps in Switzerland or some other country.

The net result was that **millions of people were defrauded directly or indirectly by the purchase of asset-backed securities whose risk and value were not verified**. Millions of people were defrauded directly or indirectly as the result of purchasing or refinancing property whose value was intentionally inflated.

All materials contained here-in are the property of the R.Sauger Company under US Copyright TX0005895316/203-12-16 or otherwise referred to as being available under the US Freedom of Information Act.

In many circumstances, the loan was not underwritten in conventional terms, and standard features like escrow accounts for insurance and taxes were excluded from the payments. Large, undisclosed and unconscionable fees and points were charged to borrowers. When these fees were combined with the Annual Percentage Rate (APR) and inflated house appraisals, these **loans were usurious in virtually every case.**

Thousands of mortgage brokers, appraisers and others involved in the process are likely to lose their licenses or otherwise receive discipline from the regulatory boards in their state or jurisdiction. We all grew up believing that a loan was money at risk to the lender and that it should be repaid, so it's difficult to accept that the banks and mortgage companies could have crafted a scheme of such monumental proportions to take advantage of that basic trust.
It also explains why this scheme has been so successful. We are basically trusting people who believed that a financial institution in this country would deal honestly with us.

Since the mortgage crisis began, the details of this scam have threatened the very existence of large financial institutions, and the financial markets themselves. The collapse of Washington Mutual, AIG, Indy-Mac Bank and others to follow is the most recent proof of how greed and lack of adherence to common sense lending has failed. When all the chips fall, who emerges as the winner? Is it possible that the failure of our monetary system was pre-planned, so that wealthy investors and foreigners could take advantage and purchase our assets at fire sale pricing?

The Mess On Wall Street And You

If you remember towards the end of George W. Bush's term in office, the Republicans and the Democrats were fighting (as usual) about the mortgage mess and who caused it. Do you also remember how at the last hour, before the Senate broke for some time off, it seemed like a national emergency for them to approve a seven hundred and fifty billion dollar bail-out package? Who, exactly, was going to be bailed out? Most people thought this would help the homeowner who was behind on a tough mortgage.

Naw, that didn't really happen. The way the bill was written, the average homeowner might get help if –and that is a big IF – their lender approved the deal. But because most homeowners had already gone into the tank with their credit, they couldn't qualify under the lending requirements of the lender. So there was no help. The government guaranteed this money to help someone. But where did the government get this money? The government had to use it's own credit. It is no wonder the U.S. has gone from being one of the largest creditor nations in the world to the largest debtor nation in such a short time.

Foreign governments now own most of our debt. What would happen if all of a sudden China decided to turn the screws? It's a scary thought. How much money do we owe Russia? Another scary thought. This entire debacle of debt scares the hell out of me, and makes me worry about our future generations. That is why I am on a mission to educate you about the system and how to improve your credit.If this thing plays out the way it looks now, the Federal Government will buy the troubled assets of some banks.

All materials contained here-in are the property of the R.Sauger Company under US Copyright TX0005895316/203-12-16 or otherwise referred to as being available under the US Freedom of Information Act.

When I say "troubled assets," I mean mortgage notes that don't exist anymore. The lenders cannot re-create them.Only the government can re-create them, once they own them. But, the trick is to first get the lenders to accept a (90%) on what the house is worth on the market today.

But the mess gets worse. Now, when the original lender closed on your loan, they did not put up any money. They got paid a commission for "table funding," or closing the deal. Once the deal was done, they were out of the loop unless they chose to "service" the loan, or be the one to collect the monthly payments, take another cut and pass the rest onto the note owner. But in many cases the original note was "securitized" or lost. The investor has been repaid because they had insurance. Didn't the government also create money to bail out AIG, the largest insurer in the country? Are you getting the picture?

So now here comes the lender, back to the trough, trying to get paid a lot of money for a loan that he doesn't have any interest in. Is this double-dipping or "unjust enrichment"? Why should the government pay this lender when he doesn't even own the note and never did own the note. This is why our mortgage industry is the mess that it is.

The Federal Reserve

Foreclosures, bankruptcies, failing business, government bailouts, more giveaway programs and more national debt. How could our financial system be in so much trouble in such a short time? Well, you may not know it, but the U.S. Dollar is privately owned by a private central bank. The owners of this bank have been responsible for instigating all the major wars and depressions in the last 100 years. They own the bank, they own the dollar and they own all the major media channels, the military industrial complex and most politicians, judges and cops. In the news, you may hear a lot about the Federal Reserve, commonly referred to "The Fed." The Federal Reserve is the central banking system of the United States, charged with providing the country's currency. Now, most Americans believe that the Fed is a part of the United States Government. This is not true!

The Federal Reserve Bank is a consortium of twelve private banks that are not part of the United States Government. The Federal Reserve System's twelve member banks are actually private banks that are owned by descendants of the, Rockefeller, J.P.Morgan family, Chase Bank and the Rothschild family. *These private banks purchase paper notes from the U.S. mint for printing cost or simply enter digital money into their computer then lend back the money plus interest to the people through member banks. The profits go into the pockets of the banks' shareholders.* The American public receives no benefit.

Please read this over and over. **The owners of the Federal Reserve Bank simply create money.** They do NOT put up any assets or collateral. When the U.S. Government approves a new zillion-dollar program, they go to the Federal Reserve and get money. Here is the catch. The Federal Reserve creates dollars, and then *loans it to the government,* and gets paid interest on those dollars. Talk about money for nothing!

All materials contained here-in are the property of the R.Sauger Company under US Copyright TX0005895316/203-12-16 or otherwise referred to as being available under the US Freedom of Information Act.

The Federal Reserve was created as a result of a secret meeting of seven men, who traveled in a private train car to Jekyl Island, Georgia in 1910. Who were these seven men? The first one was **Senator Nelson Aldrich**, who was the Republican whip in the Senate. He was the Chairman of the National Monetary Commission, the special committee that Congress had created to propose legislation to reform banking. In those days, the public was quite concerned about what was going on in the banking industry. A lot of banks were folding and people were losing their investments as banks broke their promise to guard the depositors' assets. There were "runs" on the banks, and the banks were not able to give people their money back.

People were particularly concerned about the concentration of wealth in the hands of a few large New York banks on Wall Street, called the "money trust" in those days. Quite a few politicians had been elected to office on a campaign promise to break the grip of the money trust. President Wilson was one of those politicians even though Wilson had himself been hand-picked by the money trust, financed by the money trust, and surrounded by advisors and politic cronies from the money trust.But the public didn't know this at the time, and in those days if you campaigned against the money trust you were quite likely to be elected.

This is why I like to call it "the people you love to hate" money trust. One of the main purposes of Congress' National Monetary Commission was to propose legislation that would break the grip of the money trust. In addition to being the Chairman of that Commission, Aldrich also happened to be a very important business associate of J. P. Morgan, a wealthy and powerful banker who dominated corporate finance and industry at that time. Aldrich was also the father- in-law of John D. Rockefeller, Jr., which means that eventually he became the grandfather of Nelson Rockefeller, our former vice-president. Other attendees at the meeting included **Abraham Andrew**, the Assistant Secretary of the Treasury; **Frank Vanderlip**, the President of the National City Bank of New York, the largest of all of the American banks that represented the financial interests of William Rockefeller, of the powerful Rockefeller family and the international investment firm of Kuhn, Loeb & Company; **Henry Davison**, the senior partner of the J. P. Morgan Company; **Charles Norton**, the President of the First National Bank of New York, another one of the banking giants; and **Benjamin Strong**, the head of J. P. Morgan's Banker's Trust Company, and later the first head of the Federal Reserve System.

The final attendee was **Paul Warburg**, whose knowledge of European banking made him invaluable. Paul Warburg had been born in Germany and eventually became a naturalized American citizen. He was a partner in Kuhn, Loeb & Company and was a representative of the Rothschild banking dynasty in England and France. He maintained very close working relationships throughout his entire career with his brother, Max Warburg, who was the head of the Warburg banking consortium in Germany and the Netherlands.

Paul Warburg was one of the wealthiest men in the world. In fact, those of you who are Little Orphan Annie fans will remember Daddy Warbucks, whom everyone at the time knew was a characterization of Paul Warburg. And while we're on the topic of cartoon characters, remember the game Monopoly? The mascot of the capitalist with the handlebar mustache and the cigar is supposed to be J. P. Morgan.

All materials contained here-in are the property of the R.Sauger Company under US Copyright TX0005895316/203-12-16 or otherwise referred to as being available under the US Freedom of Information Act.

These were the seven men aboard that railroad car who were at Jekyll Island. Amazing as it may seem, they represented approximately 1/4 of the wealth of the entire world. These are the men who sat around the table and created the Federal Reserve System.

How do we know? Well, Frank Vanderlip wrote an article that appeared in the Saturday Evening Post on February 9, 1935 that described the secret meeting: *"I do not feel it is any exaggeration to speak of our secret expedition to Jekyll Island as the occasion of the actual conception of what eventually became the Federal Reserve System. We were told to leave our last names behind us. We were told further that we should avoid dining together on the night of our departure. We were instructed to come one at a time and as unobtrusively as possible to the railroad terminal on the New Jersey littoral of the Hudson where Senator Aldrich's private car would be in readiness attached to the rear-end of a train to the south.*

Once aboard the private car we began to observe the taboo that had been fixed on last names. We addressed one another as Ben, Paul, Nelson and Abe. Davison and I adopted even deeper disguises abandoning our first names. On the theory that we were always right, he became Wilbur and I became Orville after those two aviation pioneers the Wright brothers. The servants and train crew may have known the identities of one or two of us, but they did not know all and it was the names of all printed together that would've made our mysterious journey significant in Washington, in Wall Street, even in London. Discovery, we knew, simply must not happen."

Why the secrecy? What was the big deal about a group of bankers getting together in private and talking about banking, or even banking legislation? Well, the answer is provided by Vanderlip himself in the same article. He said that, *"If it were to be exposed publicly that our particular group had gotten together and written a banking bill, that bill would have no chance whatever of passage by Congress."*

Why not? Because the bill was to break the grip of the money trust -- and the text of the bill had just been written by the money trust itself. Had that fact been known at the get-go, we would never have had a Federal Reserve System, because as Vanderlip himself said in the article, it would have had no chance at all of passage by Congress. It was essential to keep that whole thing a secret at the time, and it has largely remained an "open secret" even to this day. It's an open secret because anybody can go to the library and dig this information out – but it is certainly not taught in textbooks! You won't know this from reading the official literature from the Federal Reserve System – because that is like asking the fox to build the henhouse and install the security system.

Today, the Primary Owners of the Federal Reserve Bank Are:

1. Rothschild's of London and Berlin
2. Lazard Brothers of Paris
3. Israel Moses Seaf of Italy
4. Kuhn, Loeb & Co. of Germany and New York
5. Warburg & Company of Hamburg, Germany
6. Lehman Brothers of New York

All materials contained here-in are the property of the R.Sauger Company under US Copyright TX0005895316/203-12-16 or otherwise referred to as being available under the US Freedom of Information Act.

7. Goldman, Sachs of New York
8. Rockefeller Brothers of New York

These banks literally own exclusive rights to the dollar. For them money does not grow on trees -- it comes from making an entry in their books. The private ownership of the U.S. Dollar is by far the greatest crime of the century. In Aaron Russo's must-see movie *From Freedom to Fascism*, he asks Congressman Ron Paul, *"So the Federal Reserve is actually an illegal entity functioning within the Federal Government?"* Ron Paul's response is, *"It's illegal. And what we have given to this so-called agency is the authority to counterfeit money."*

This system costs the United States hundreds of billions of dollars every year, and holds its people in a constant state of debt. Sometimes the Federal Reserve Bank pays an arbitrary 'franchise fee' to the U.S. government to keep the politicians paid off, and there have been assassination attempts on every President who attempted to eliminate private national banks in the U.S.

The privately-held Federal Reserve Bank has never been audited, and does not pay any income tax on their astonishing income. The Federal Reserve is supposed to bring stability to the economy, but it is behind almost every major market crash and war can be attributed to the Federal Reserve Bank, including the Great Depression, World War I, World War II, and the Gulf War. By controlling our money supply, the Federal Reserve System can, and does, control inflation and deflation. Think about this! Let's say that on Friday the Federal Government owed one billion dollars to other countries because our balance of trade was upside down. (In other words, we imported more stuff like oil and manufactured goods, and exported a lot less.) Hear the cries of the affected workers now! So if the Federal Reserve simply creates more money over the weekend, our balance of trade will be increased because value of the dollar will drop.

Credit Card Companies

Remember a president by the name of Jimmy Carter? He was a peanut farmer from Plains, Georgia who was a brilliant engineer and a military man but not the best numbers man we ever had in the White House. In fact he had a little brother named Billie who dreamed of being a "beer baron". Do you remember when he came out with "Billie Beer?" Anybody got any of those collector items lying around?

In the fifties, sixties and seventies, we always could borrow money from the neighborhood loan shark. If you borrowed $100 bucks, you simply paid him back $120 bucks. Very convenient. He was making an instant 20%. That was called loan sharking and when he went to collect using strong-arm tactics, it was considered extortion. By the time Jimmy Carter left office, he had virtually put the loan sharks out of business. This was a decent thing to do, and I compliment him for that. But the reason that they were going out of business is that by the time President Carter had left the White House, prime interest rates had risen to around 24%!!!!

All materials contained here-in are the property of the R.Sauger Company under US Copyright TX0005895316/203-12-16 or otherwise referred to as being available under the US Freedom of Information Act.

This high rate virtually put the *"kibosh"* on the local loan shark and enabled the credit card companies to start charging 24% interest. I have heard of interest rates on some credit cards as being as high as 36%.

When you couple the lack of fiscal responsibility of Jimmy Carter and you combine that with the State of North Dakota's very innocent move to remove usury rates in North Dakota, the movement West started. This was the "gold rush" re-incarnated. Big banks, like Citi, Chase and others moved their credit card operations to North Dakota and soon we saw the emergence of .36% interest on credit cards. I can say with all sincerity, that anyone that has to pay .36% interest today WILL NEVER PAY OF THAT CARD. It is an impossibility unless you win the lotto.

This is the single most "social cancer" that we as Americans have to endure. Sure, you say, just get your credit scores higher. But, do you think that the credit card companies want the general public to have higher credit scores? I don't know what you are smoking, but all indications today point to a "collusion" between the credit reporting agencies and the creditors to keep you in CREDIT PRISON. I say "GET OUT OF CREDIT PRISON".

If a credit card company wants to steal from you, they don't even have to show up at your house. They just take it from you and you don't even know it. How? Well, with today's ability to raise your interest rates whenever you are late, over limit or even have another account with issues, **they simply raise your rates, and steal another $100 from you – without even using a gun**. Do I have your attention now?

If, I, showed up at your door on Friday night after you got your paycheck and I asked you to give me $200.00: would you? You most probably would throw me off of the porch. Well, Charlie, take a lesson in "economics from the streets". I don't have to show up at your house. I don't even need a gun to steal the $200.00 from you. Hell, I'll just go to the office instead of driving to your house and raise your interest rate. And guess what? You can't do a damned thing about it. Who are you going to complain to? There are NO CREDIT COPS. Get real. Don't you understand by now that when you don't care about credit, the "white crime" pros will just take it from you and smile.

Collection Agencies

A collection agency is a **for-profit business** that pursues payments owed by individuals or businesses. Some of collection agencies operate as an agent of the creditor, and receive a fee or percentage of the total amount owed. Other agencies, called debt buyers, purchase the debts for a fraction of their value, and then still try to collect the full amount owed. There are many cases where a group of lawyers will get together and pool their money to buy "time-barred debt" from lenders for a few cents on the dollar. When they send you a letter on their legal stationery telling you that they now own your debt, they have the ability to strike fear into your heart.

All materials contained here-in are the property of the R.Sauger Company under US Copyright TX0005895316/203-12-16 or otherwise referred to as being available under the US Freedom of Information Act.

Creditors use collection agencies so that they can remove debts from their records, and write off the debts as a loss to receive certain tax benefits. And, they sell debts that are no longer legally collectible to debt buyers – even though they only get cents on the dollar, to them it's better than nothing.

Debt collectors who work on commission are highly motivated to convince you to pay the debt. The first time they call you, they may play "good cop", and try to build rapport and convince you to pay some or all of the debt. If that doesn't work, they may switch to "bad cop", using threatening language or dirty tricks. They will do **whatever it takes** to get you to give them some money –*ANY MONEY* – because that's the only way they make a profit on the account. Third-party collections agencies are regulated by the Fair Debt Collection Practices Act (FDCP), which is administered by the Federal Trade Commission (FTC.) While there are strict guidelines designed to protect consumers from abusive treatment, my experience has been that debt collectors blatantly ignore the rules – and usually get away with it.

Why Would "The System" *Want* Me to Have Bad Credit?

Imagine that you are a banker who is interested in investing two million dollars by providing consumer credit cards, and that you are sitting in front a room full of 100 people who want to apply for one of your cards. Now imagine that you have divided the room into two equal groups – on the left are the people who have poor credit, and on the right are the people who have good credit. If, you were going to offer one million dollars to the group on the left with good credit, and the other million dollars to the group on the right with poor credit. *Which group do you think would be the better investment for you?*

Before we answer that question, I want to explain to you the **Rule of 72**. This is something that is not taught at Wharton School of Business, Harvard or any Ivy League School. Heck, they don't even teach it in progressive California. I learned about the Rule of 72 on the streets of Detroit when I was a kid running mutual slips for the Italian gambling syndicate. The Rule of 72 is a way to easily calculate how many years it will take to double your original investment, by dividing the percent interest into the number 72. Here's how it works. Suppose that your Aunt Rose had $10,000, and since she's a smart woman, she put it into the bank to grow a nice nest egg. Let's say that the bank is paying Aunt Rose 4% interest on her passbook savings.

Take out your pencil or calculator and divide 72 by 4. Well, without waiting for you, the answer is 18. That means that it takes 18 years for Aunt Rose's $10,000 to double. While the bank had her money, they loaned it right back to her to buy a car at 12% interest (another great deal). Now divide 12 into 72 and you will see that the bank doubled Aunt Rose's money in just six years, and they didn't have to save all of their lives to get that money.

So let's put this into perspective. When a credit card company is charging you 24% interest, just divide 24 into 72 and you will see that the credit card companies are doubling your hard-earned money in three years. Don't believe it? Just do the numbers. Now let's get back to room full of people and your two million dollar investment.

All materials contained here-in are the property of the R.Sauger Company under US Copyright TX0005895316/203-12-16 or otherwise referred to as being available under the US Freedom of Information Act.

Let's assume that you are going to charge 8% interest to the group with good credit, and 24% interest to the group with poor credit. How long will it take you to double your money on each group?

Group 1 - Good Credit:
72 / 8 = double your investment in 9 years $1,000,000 @ 8% after 9 years = $2,000,000

Group 2 - Damaged Credit:
72 / 24= double your investment in 3 years $1,000,000 @ 24% after 3 years = $2,000,000
As a banker, you can double your money three times as quickly with the group of bad credit. And in the space of just 9 years, you could make four times more interest on the group with poor credit than you could with the group with good credit.

Group 2 - Damaged Credit:
Your $1,000,000 investment at 24% interest: At the end of three years = $2,000,000
At the end of six years = $4,000,000 At the end of nine years = $8,000,000

Even considering the fact that the group with poor credit might not make payments, group two is a far better return. Let's say that half of the people in Group 2 never repay their credit card balance. At the end of nine years, the group with good credit would return $2 million, while the group with bad credit would return half of $8 million, or a total of $4 million – still double the return. If you were the bank, which group would you choose? **Now you see why folks with damaged credit are great investments.**

There is also something very significant about this. Ask yourself, why won't the banks or credit card companies give us some help to raise our credit scores? Well, if it took you longer than a minute to answer this question after reading this section, you have to go back to school. The **reason no one will help you is because you represent a bottom line profit** to them and if they helped you to raise your credit scores it would cost them significant profits.

"Naw, Regis you cannot be serious!" Well, I have seen time and time again the horror stories of how folks who miss just one payment see their interest rates skyrocket from 9.9% to 24% overnight. Fair? Not at all. It is simply business. Okay, get a cup of coffee or a glass of your favorite. Let's look at what the US Government has to say about the issue that plagues over (90%) of all credit reports. This is important for you and we will be talking about this many times throughout the program. I believe this is the *most important* issue on all credit reports.

6. THE LAW IS ON YOUR SIDE..

Fair Credit Reporting Act

The Fair Credit Reporting Act (FCRA) is a federal law that regulates the collection, dissemination and use of consumer credit information. It was originally passed in 1970, and is enforced by the Federal Trade Commission (FTC).

All materials contained here-in are the property of the R.Sauger Company under US Copyright TX0005895316/203-12-16 or otherwise referred to as being available under the US Freedom of Information Act.

I want you to become acquainted with Section 623(a)(5) of the Fair Credit Reporting Act. In this section, it explains that the seven-year period of reporting derogatory entries on your credit files begins when the account was first late and never got caught up. This is very powerful stuff. Even your brother-in-law who seems so smart doesn't know this. In street talk it means that when you missed a payment and never got caught up, the month and year that you were first late begins the start of your credit prison sentence. Under the Fair Debt Collection Practices Act, it is a violation of Federal Law, when a creditor/furnisher of information ages your account by adding time to it.

In my workshops and seminars, I always stress that the single most important question to ask yourself is *"What was the first date I stopped paying on this account and NEVER got caught up?"* Your sentence to "credit prison" has a maximum of seven years, and the clock starts on the date you first became delinquent. After seven years, your credit returns back to normal (providing you are paying bills on time.)

A 2003 amendment to the FCRA entitles you to receive one free credit report per year from the big three credit bureaus. The bureaus are responsible for verifying any information that you dispute. You can request your free report by telephone, by mail, or through the government-authorized web site www.annualcreditreport.com

Statute of Limitations and Time-Barred Debts

The Statute of limitations (SOL) in your state determines how many years a creditor can legally collect before the debt is classified as **"time-barred."** Once an open-ended debt becomes time-barred *the consumer legally no longer owes the debt*. Open-ended debts include department store cards, credit cards and gas cards. The Federal Truth In Lending Act is very specific in defining exactly what OPEN END DEBT is.

They are called open-ended because your balance changes month to month to include your most recent purchases and payments. You do not know in advance what the payment will be each month. An auto loan, on the other hand, is a fixed contract with regular payments, and therefore is NOT an open-ended debt. In order to calculate when your open-ended debt becomes time-barred, you must know the date you stopped making payments, or as Section 623 (a)(5) of the Fair Credit Reporting Act calls it, the "commencement of the initial delinquency." *The date that you were first late on the account and never got caught up triggers the beginning of the Statue of Limitations for collection.*

Once your account goes past the SOL date, the banks have virtually given up hope of collection and will take whatever they can get. Junk Debt buyers will purchase big amounts of this debt from banks and credit card companies for pennies on the dollar, and hope to frighten the average person into paying a portion of what you *think* you still owe. What an ulcerative business.

All materials contained here-in are the property of the R.Sauger Company under US Copyright TX0005895316/203-12-16 or otherwise referred to as being available under the US Freedom of Information Act.

I must, however, caution you about this defense. If you are taken to court for a time-barred debt, **you must show up to defend yourself**, or at least answer the lawsuit (complaint) by saying that your defense is that the debt is time-barred. If you show up or respond with proof that the debt is time-barred, any judge will throw the case out.

But listen up carefully – **know the law**. If you fail to show up, or fail to answer the complaint, that shark will win a deficiency judgment against you. By being lazy or avoiding the issue, you now legally owe something that you did *not* have to pay. These greedy attorneys and bottom feeders know that the average person is either intimidated by the thought of being in a courtroom, or doesn't care and won't respond. They depend on your complacency.

HEED MY WORDS , and defend you rights. Find out what the statute of limitations laws are in your state (see the Appendix for a complete listing.) *If you are past the statute of limitations, you simply don't owe the money any longer.*

Fair Debt Collection Practices Act

The Fair Debt Collection Practices Act (FDCPA) is a United States statute that was added in 1978 as part of the Consumer Credit Protection Act. The FDCPA is designed to eliminate abusive consumer debt collection practices, and provide consumers with a way to ensure their debt information is correct, and to dispute it when it's not. This act is also enforced by the FTC. **The FDCPA prohibits certain types of "abusive and deceptive" conduct when collecting debts,** including:

1. Contacting you by telephone before 8:00 AM or after 9:00 PM, local time.

2. Contacting you in any way after you tell them in writing that you wish no further contact or that you refuse to pay the debt (with exceptions).

3. Contacting you at your place of employment after you tell them in writing that this is not acceptable.

4. Using deception to collect the debt, including impersonating an attorney or law enforcement officer.

When the police arrest someone, they are required by law to advise that person of their rights, called their Miranda rights. You've seen this on TV a hundred times: *"You have the right to remain silent..."* Well, when a collector or creditor contacts you by phone or mail, they must use the following words, what I call a "mini Miranda": *"This is an attempt to collect a debt. You have thirty days from the date that you receive this notice to dispute any portion of the debt. If you fail to respond within those thirty days, this office can only **assume** that the debt is valid and can pursue legal means to collect."*

All materials contained here-in are the property of the R.Sauger Company under US Copyright TX0005895316/203-12-16 or otherwise referred to as being available under the US Freedom of Information Act.

The first thing to remember is that if a collector calls you, and they do not begin the call by saying these *exact* words, they have already violated your rights, and you may have grounds to have the collector fined. If you tell the collector that they you are recording the call (even if you're not), it's often enough to stop the harassment. (See Chapter 8 for how to stop nasty calls and letters.)

The second thing to note is the wording of this statement: assuming the debt is valid is different than proving that the debt is valid. "Assuming that the debt is valid" is not the same as legal proof that the debt is valid. **Under the FDCPA, you may request proof of your debt at any time** (even after the 30 days are up). The burden of proof lies with the debt collector, not with you. By law, you may demand that the debt collector provide adequate proof that:

- the debt is actually yours
- the amount of the debt is correct
- the debt is still collectible under the statute of limitations

The collector must, by law, stop all attempts to collect the debt until they have sent a sufficient response to your request for validation. And if the collector is unable to provide proof that the amount or date are correct, you may be able to have the derogatory item deleted from your credit report. You can learn more about his in Chapter 16.

Truth In Lending Act

The Truth in Lending Act (TILA) was enacted by Congress 1968 to protect consumers from predatory lending practices. To enable consumers to shop for credit, **The Truth in Lending Act requires clear disclosure of key terms and all costs in the lending arrangement.** You may be able to perform a **TILA Forensic Audit** to discover if your mortgage violates the Truth in Lending Act. A TILA audit must be performed by a qualified person, such as a mortgage professional who is able to review your loan documents and search for material violations. There are too many different kinds of material violations to list here, but one of the most common is called a *"liar's loan."* This is where someone has insufficient income to qualify for a loan, but the broker or processor "fudges" the numbers so that the borrower qualifies and they get their points.

Another common material violation occurs when the closing agent fails to provide you with two copies of a HUD brochure explaining your rights under Federal Law. Even, if you were the only one on the loan application and your husband was just on the Deed, he must be provided the same materials. Most times this does not happen and this is a material violation. To be eligible for a TILA audit, the home must be your primary residence and not an investment property, and you must have re-financed within the last three years. If you uncover TILA violations, you will need legal representation in court. For more on TILA Audits, see Chapter 13.

All materials contained here-in are the property of the R.Sauger Company under US Copyright TX0005895316/203-12-16 or otherwise referred to as being available under the US Freedom of Information Act.

The regulation implementing The Truth In Lending Act is known as **Regulation Z**, and provides for a variety of collection methods. Under Regulation Z, a bank must either charge off a debt or place it for collection after it has been delinquent for 150 days (or approximately 5 months).

This means that if the creditor has charged off your account and therefore received tax relief, they can no longer carry the amount you owe on their books as an account receivable. They also cannot report to credit reporting agencies that you have a "balance owed".

The only thing that they *can* show on your credit report is that the account was "charged off" and has "zero balance". If you see a "balance owed" on your credit report at the same time that account has been turned over to a collector, that is a derogatory entry that MUST be deleted.

Unfortunately, without any credit cops the CRAs rarely respond to requests to correct your account. In Chapter 16 I describe how you can get their attention by threatening a small claims lawsuit.

Picture yourself coming home on Friday night after cashing your paycheck. What if I, a total stranger, showed up at the door and demanded that you give me a hundred bucks? You would probably tell me I'm crazy, and to go away. But what if I told you I was a BILL COLLECTOR and scared the daylights out of you with stories about ruining your credit or sending you to jail? No doubt you might hand over the hundred dollars just to make me go away.

Debt collection is a very profitable game, and many companies specialize in fishing in these shark-infested waters. Be careful – if a collection agency is hell-bent on getting some money from you they will try anything! Since you are in collections:

- They can guess that you are receiving lot of harassing phone calls and official-looking letters from law offices.

- They know that you're afraid to talk to them because they sound mean.

- They pray that you will pay them something – anything – to make them go away.

The main reason so many consumers are afraid of bill collectors is they think that the collector knows more about them, and that it is the collector who has the law on his side. Nothing could be further from the truth. ***The law is on your side.*** If a collector even comes close to breaking the laws on collections, they are subject to a fine of $1,000.

All materials contained here-in are the property of the R.Sauger Company under US Copyright TX0005895316/203-12-16 or otherwise referred to as being available under the US Freedom of Information Act.

Collectors Play Games.

Believe me when I tell you that there is high turnover among professional bill collectors, and as a result, most of them are ignorant of the laws. Why? Well, would you stay at a job where you had to peddle misery for eight hours a day? Now combine that ignorance with greed for high commissions and the wonderful, friendly personality that they all seem to have, and you can see how they are able to build a wall of insulation and continue to harass people.

They know that you won't fight. Who would you complain to? There are no "credit cops." That's right, you heard me correctly. **There are no credit cops.** If you have a noisy neighbor, you can simply call the police station and file a disturbance against them. But when a bill collector calls and begins to insult you, most people just don't know where to turn.

Collectors often lie about marking your account favorably if you send them money. Often a law firm or collection agency will tell you that if you send them a certain amount of money, they will mark the account your credit report favorably. All of this is "crap" and "garbage" – the only thing these weasels are interested in is intimidating you to pay some money.

7. DIRTY TRICKS ....

Aging Your Account

As I mentioned before, according to the Fair Credit Reporting Act, ***a negative entry can only show up on your credit report for seven years from the date of first delinquency*** (as long as you have been paying your bills on time since then.) Many collections agencies are "sleeping at the switch," and do not know the actual date of your first delinquency. Without this information, they often post the date when they were assigned the account as the opening date, which could be years later. This is called aging the account.

Why don't the creditors provide the correct information? Imagine that I'm a creditor who sentenced you to credit prison for seven years, and let's say that six years and eleven months have passed. Do you think I want to let you out of the "yoke" of paying high interest rates once and for all? After all, when you once again have good credit, you won't be paying that 24% interest. When a collection agency ages your account, it's as if they sneaked into your cell in the middle of the night and added four years to your credit prison sentence without your knowing it. You should be livid! But they do this kind of thing every day. You can find out about this specific issue in Chapter 16, Cleaning up Your Credit Report.

Aging an account is a violation of your federal rights, and it carries a mandated fine of $1,000 payable to you, if you are the victim. For a great example of justice in action, see the story in Chapter 16 about how the Federal Trade Commission fined a company named NCO to the tune of $1.5 million for re-aging the date of first delinquency on consumers' accounts.

All materials contained here-in are the property of the R.Sauger Company under US Copyright TX0005895316/203-12-16 or otherwise referred to as being available under the US Freedom of Information Act.

Restarting Your Credit Prison Clock

Most collection agencies have their computer systems already programmed to recognize when an account that has been either charged off or placed for collection has been delinquent for exactly six and a half years, a few months from the statute of limitations (SOL.) About this time, you may receive an extremely friendly letter from them that says something like, *"Greetings from your new friends down here at Misery Bill Collectors. We know you would like to settle this past bill that you owe to Lifetime Television Repair, and we would like to help you. If you will send in a token payment of only $20 to show your good faith, we will work with you to settle this account in a friendly manner".*

Don't fall for this trick! The bill collectors are not trying to help you – they're trying to re-start the seven- year clock on your debt. They are trying to get new "activity" on the account. Sending them a letter does not count as activity – but making a payment or partial payment does count as activity. BUT, remember 623(A-5) of the Fair Credit Reporting Act. It was specific. "The seven year period of reporting commences when an account was first late and NEVER got caught up". So, there it is. Whatever any collection agency, attorney, advisor or nut tells you, it is in writing and it IS FEDERAL LAW. Don't fall for this crap of "restarting the clock".

Junk Debt Buyers

There are a number of for-profit companies that purchase unpaid debts that have already been written off, or that are beyond the Statue of Limitations for collection, meaning the original creditor can no longer attempt to collect. (You can read more about this in Chapter 6.) Many times a group of attorneys will pool their resources and purchase blocks of junk debt together.

These groups purchase millions of past-due debt for pennies on the dollar. For example, your $10,000 credit card debt that is beyond the Statute of Limitations might cost them $300.00. Once they buy your account, they start with the phone calls and letters.

Sometimes they say they want to "help" you in settling this debt. They offer you a 50% discount if you pay them immediately. Often they threaten you into giving them anything you can afford. Do they really want to "help" you? Well, figure it out. If you pay them the "half" that they're asking for, they make $5,000 on their $300.00 investment. WOW!!! And this is on a debt that you might not legally owe.

Now, up until you learned about what the **SOL** means, you probably have gotten one of those "amusing" collection letters from the local "happy, daffy collectors" at Rookum, Shaftum and Howe Law office. Wow, the nerve of these guys that drive their little kids to school, volunteer for the choir directors job on Sundays and most probably have been selected as the Man of the Month by the local "Jolly Do-Gooder Club".

All materials contained here-in are the property of the R.Sauger Company under US Copyright TX0005895316/203-12-16 or otherwise referred to as being available under the US Freedom of Information Act.

But here they are, just like a school of sharks, circling for that "financial blood" that they can extract from those folks that just haven't had a chance to understand their legal rights.

In these situations we can see how that local law firm has taken aim on their having knowledge of the law and how they can use it to mentally strong-arm you out of money.

Junk debt buyers, most of which most are owned or managed by lawyers, assume that most people who owe the money don't have a clue about the Statute of limitations and how it affects them.

8. DEALING WITH HARRASSMENT..................................

Remember Your Rights

Bill collectors' sole purpose is to get money from you, in any way they can. They will try every dirty trick in the book, both legal and illegal. Most people do not understand their rights, and are easily tricked into making payments to these sharks. Verify and Validate - You may receive a letter that says if you fail to respond in 30 days, the collector can assume the debt is valid and pursue legal action. **Remember, the burden of proof is upon them!** At any time, even after the 30 days have passed, you still have the right to:

1) Ask for a complete accounting history of your debt, and

2) Dispute the amount of the debt, and on what date the account became delinquent. In many cases, the collectors do not have this information. You can read more about this in Chapter 16.

Communications In Writing Only – You can request, in writing, that all future communications about your debt be in writing. Any phone calls from collectors after this request is received are in violation of the Fair Debt Collection Practices Act.

Statute of Limitations – If your date of first delinquency has occurred longer than the Statute of limitations for your state, the debt is time-barred, and not legally collectible. Junk Debt collectors will try to trick you into paying any amount. You must know the first date you were delinquent in order to learn if your account is time-barred.

How to Stop Nasty Letters

Many collections agencies will pay a greedy attorney for the use of his/her legal stationery. Why? Because, it makes the collections letter look very threatening, and you are more likely to cough up some money as a result. We have seen hundreds of letters where these creeps use the local attorney's stationery in the hopes of scaring you. And believe me, it usually works. They get money from the intimidated consumer and the greedy attorney gets a cut for simply allowing someone to use his office or letterhead.

All materials contained here-in are the property of the R.Sauger Company under US Copyright TX0005895316/203-12-16 or otherwise referred to as being available under the US Freedom of Information Act.

The law says that an attorney must have complete knowledge of your case, which means they have spent a minimum of 30 minutes reviewing the file. If the attorney simply handed over their official-looking letterhead to a bill collector, that is a violation of The Fair Debt Collection Practices Act.

One of these crooked attorneys was brought before a federal judge, who asked how much time he spent on each file before a collections letter was sent out on his letterhead. The attorney told the judge that it took him at least 30 minutes to look at each file. The judge did some quick math and said, "Well, according to your calculations, you could review no more than two cases per hour. At that rate, working a ten hour day, you would review twenty cases per day; at five days a week you could review forty cases each week, or one hundred cases each month. So why is it that your office sent out almost three thousand collection letters last month with your signature?".

The law office and the attorney were found guilty of violating the Fair Debt Collections Practices Act and fined over $350,000 dollars. If the letter you receive is signed by a lawyer who puts "Esquire" or the abbreviation "Esq." after his or her name, you must assume it's a valid letter, and treat it accordingly. However, if the letter is not signed by an attorney, then you may want to investigate.

How to Stop Nasty Phone Calls

I'll just bet that at some point you started receiving some pretty nasty phone calls. Have you ever wondered what type of "fanged-tooth creature" is on the other end of the line? Let's say the collector said something like, *"This is Mr. Bad, and I want to know when you are going to pay the money that you owe me!"* Let's look at this opening statement.

First of all, you never bought anything from Mr. Bad. So where does he get off asking "when are you going to pay me the money that you owe me"?

Second, Mr. Bad really put his foot in his mouth when he failed to read you your "mini-Miranda" rights. By federal law, Mr. Bad is mandated to start the conversation by saying: *"My name is Mr. Bad. I am a bill collector working with/for ABC Company. This is an attempt to collect a debt. If you do not agree with the amount we are collecting, you have thirty days from today to notify us of your dispute. If you fail to respond within that thirty days, we can only assume that the debt is valid and we can proceed to using any legal remedy available."*

Mr. Bad clearly failed to read you your rights, a violation that is punishable with a fine of $1,000. **Receiving nasty phone calls from collectors can be extremely stressful.** These Secret Service rejects think that because they have the power of the telephone that they can control you and manipulate you into saying something that would be to their favor. Why would you send money to a complete stranger on the phone, a person you don't know, and never bought anything from?

All materials contained here-in are the property of the R.Sauger Company under US Copyright TX0005895316/20312-16 or otherwise referred to as being available under the US Freedom of Information Act.

Take this piece of advice from an old man who has been there and done that: hang up! That's correct, you can hang up at any time. In fact, at my workshops I often help folks practice how to properly answer a telephone call from a collection agency. (Riiiiiiiiing... Riiiiiiiiing...) "Hello?" "This is Mr. Bad, and I'm a bill collector..." (Click) **You can hang up the phone at any time.** Period. Don't make conversation, don't try to chat or ask him/her how they are feeling. You are nothing more to them than a sucker, and they will try to get money any way they can. If you feel that you have a special gift, and that you might get some useful information by talking to a bill collector, then go ahead – but proceed with extreme caution. The best strategy is to ask more questions than they do. *If they don't answer your questions, hang up.*

Here are examples of questions to ask a bill collector:

1. Can you provide a complete record of my account?
2. Are you licensed in my State?
3. What is your social security number?
4. How old are you?
5. Why are you calling me while I am eating dinner?
6. What company pays your paycheck?
7. Are you on commission?
8. Can you tell me when I made my last payment?
9. Can you tell me how you calculated what you claim I owe?

Get the picture? By the time you have asked all of these questions, the collector will become frustrated. If he gets nasty, that is when you hang up. There is no other choice.

To stop calls at work, you must first tell them in writing that your employer does not permit outside phone calls. By law, they must stop calling you after they receive this notification. If you do receive additional calls at work after providing a written request to stop, you have two options:

1. **To stop the calls immediately,** tell them that you are recording this phone call, and that they are in violation of federal law. Most bill collectors do not want their voice recorded, so that usually does the trick!
2. **If you want to file a complaint** (and have them be fined $1,000), you need to collect evidence. Don't stop them from calling! Instead, create a phone log to record all calls that you receive from a collector, which contains dates, times, caller's names, and notes on what was discussed.
3. This log may be admissible in court.

To stop calls at home, I can recommend a variety of methods.

1. The simplest one is to **screen your calls** with an answering machine or service. When you record your message, simply tell callers they are being recorded. This way your voice mail doesn't fill up with nasty messages.

All materials contained here-in are the property of the R.Sauger Company under US Copyright TX0005895316/203-12-16 or otherwise referred to as being available under the US Freedom of Information Act.

2. You can **tell the collector that you are recording the call**. Most of them do not want their shady methods to be caught on tape, and the calls will stop.
3. You can **notify the collector in writing** to cease and desist from making any phone calls to you, and *from that point they must communicate with you in writing*. If they contact you by phone after this notification, they are in violation of the Fair Debt Collection Practices Act, and subject to a $1,000 fine.
4. This is not a hard thing to do. Simply sit down and send them a short letter that says, *"Do not call me any more. You must communicate with me in writing only. Your continued calls will be recorded and used against you in my seeking all legal remedies under federal law."*
5. If they call before 8AM or after 9PM (your local time), they are in violation of the Fair Debt Collection Practices act, also punishable by a $1,000 fine. Do not let them make the excuse that "well, it's only 7:30 PM where I am." Won't fly, don't buy. If you tell them you are recording the call, they will usually hang up.
6. Remember that there is no law that says you must talk to them on the phone. **You may hang up at any time.**

A single mom named Pauline came to one of my classes, and told us that because of the tactics of bill collectors, she was a nervous wreck and couldn't eat or sleep. I really felt sorry for her! The only thing she wanted was a home for her kids, a chance to settle her debts and to be left alone.

Now, these heartless characters, both male and female, knew that she was "fresh meat" and had no ability to stand up to them. We simply instructed her to stop at K-Mart on the way home and pick up a $15 telephone answering machine and record this exact message: "Hello, this is Pauline Smith, thank you for calling me. Your call is extremely important, and is being *recorded*, so please leave a nice message and I will get back to you soon."

In most states, you can record someone's phone call as long as you let them know they are being recorded. Well, after placing this message on the machine, Pauline was astounded; the only messages she gets are loud "clicks". In other words, the collectors did not leave their name or number. They simply hung up. Wonder why?

The best way to catch them in any illegal is to actually record the call. You can buy an inexpensive voice recorder, and simply hold it to your phone's receiver. (Laws about notifying the caller that they are being recorded vary by state.) And it's always a good idea to keep a journal of all collection calls – the caller, the date, the time, and what was discussed – as this can be good evidence for future actions. In order to find out exactly who you are dealing with, just pretend that you need their address and company information in order to send payment. I want you to know that you really can get rid of these characters. *Remember, the law is on your side.*

THIS IS IMPORTANT: Never, ever, give your checking account information to anyone. I have seen many cases where a collector convinces the debtor to hand over their checking account and routing numbers so he can get the money more quickly and easily. They *promise* to take only the amount that you discuss.

All materials contained here-in are the property of the R.Sauger Company under US Copyright TX0005895316/203-12-16 or otherwise referred to as being available under the US Freedom of Information Act.

Don't fall for their claims that they care about you, or that they are an honorable person with your best interests at heart! These are professionals who are trained to extract money from you any way they can. Surprised? Don't be. You are like hundreds of thousands of consumers who believe there is a tooth fairy. Once a collector has entry into your bank account, believe me, they **will take all of your money and cause you to be overdrawn**. And there will be nothing you can do to get that money back. If you have already given out your checking account information, there may still be time to undo the damage.

Quickly close the bank account and open a new one. If you choose to do this, be sure to update all other legitimate billers, to ensure you don't miss any other payments. **Beware of phone calls from a "lawyer."** Most lawyers prefer to communicate in writing, so phone calls are highly suspicious. And don't be fooled by someone who claims that they can have you arrested if you don't pay by a certain time that day. A warrant for your arrest must be signed by a judge, a bureaucratic process that is rarely completed in one day.

If you're suspicious, tell them that you know that impersonating an officer of the court is a federal crime and that you are now recording the call. Can they please repeat what they just said? You will most likely hear the click as they hang up.

One of my workshop students in Florida had been getting nasty phone calls from a bill collector. She was so distraught that she went to the local police station to file a complaint. The corporal on the desk apparently had experienced similar situations with his family, and offered to help the girl. She called the bill collector and told him that she was at the police station and that the corporal wanted to talk to him and record his voice. The collector said, "Oh, I have been through these scams before. That guy you have acting as a police officer is probably your brother-in-law. That won't work lady. So you either pay up by 5:00 PM or I will have you arrested".

I would love to have seen the look on this guy's face when the corporal took the telephone. Then a strange thing happened – the debt went away and she got an apology from the original creditor. Had she known her rights, she could have sued for a substantial amount in court. That is the most serious violation of the Fair Debt Collection Practices Act I have ever heard of.

I also had a personal experience with a law firm in Atlanta, Georgia. My son was late on a credit card and he got a letter from a "law firm" threatening legal action. Right after the letter arrived, I got a phone call from a man at the law firm who thought I was my son. (He asked for "Mr. Sauger" and I confirmed that I am, indeed, Mr. Sauger.) This so-called lawyer informed me that "if I didn't send a money order to his office by 5:00 PM, there would be a warrant out for my arrest."

First I said, "Gee, I sure don't want to go to jail! Could you please give me the address and name of the person to whom I would have the money order made out?" Then I asked this person how he could have me arrested by 5:00 pm without going before a judge.

All materials contained here-in are the property of the R.Sauger Company under US Copyright TX0005895316/203-12-16 or otherwise referred to as being available under the US Freedom of Information Act.

Well, he was caught off guard and I knew he needed some "mumbling room". He had no idea who he was dealing with, and he really thought I was my son. I asked him how he could have an arrest warrant before a violation of the law was determined by the court. He again didn't know what to say.

So I unloaded on him. I said, "I have recorded your conversation and will use it in my upcoming lawsuit against you and your office for violating the Fair Debt Collection Practices and for threatening to arrest me without even having gotten a warrant from the Judge!"

Talk about a monkey scrambling for the bananas! This guy was frantic. He asked again, "Are you Mr. Sauger?" I reassured him that I was indeed "Mr. Sauger". But this time I asked the blooming idiot why he was impersonating an officer of the court and threatening me with arrest without the authority of the court. The letter was the first mistake and the phone call was what took it over the top. Irony is really poetry in motion. We caught this collection agency law firm and their crooked lawyer with their hand in the cookie jar.

They were using a scam to scare an unsuspecting person, but boy, they didn't know who they were dealing with this time. In the end, the account was deleted from my son's credit files and an apology was furnished from the original creditor for the collector's activities.

When Was the Account First Late?

Let's put on our common sense hats here. The single most important piece of information you need to have is *the date that the account was first late, and never got caught up.* Why is this so important? Well, if you have this information, you might just find out that these "zoo keepers" are attempting to collect on a debt you might just not legally owe, because it is past the statute of limitations (SOL) for your state.

Please read this, and read it again, and then read it one more time. ***The single most important question to ask is, "when was the account first late and never got caught up"?*** The only way you can determine this date is to get it in writing. A bill collector who calls you does not want to help you. He just wants money.

Will this sewer disciple give you the date your account was first late over the telephone? I don't think so. If he does, I have a bridge to sell you. He probably doesn't even have a clue what information you are trying to get. Your only courses of action are to either ***hang up***, or tell him that you will ***communicate only in writing***. The **ONLY** way to determine the date you were first late is to get a full copy of your payment record. This is tricky, and many creditors do not have these records. You have the right to validate the amount of your debt – even if it is off by only five cents. But there is no way for you to dispute any portion of the debt without being able to reviewing the entire accounting.

All materials contained here-in are the property of the R.Sauger Company under US Copyright TX0005895316/203-12-16 or otherwise referred to as being available under the US Freedom of Information Act.

The typical Joseph Six-pack simply takes the bill collector at his word, trusting that whatever in the guy's computer must be correct. Remember, what these collectors tell you is usually wrong.

But there is a second and very important reason to ask for your records under The Fair Debt Collection Practices Act. **Bill collectors usually cannot produce your full record; and if they can't prove the debt, they are required by law to delete it from your credit report.** When these sharks know they cannot produce the records, they will next try to "get what they can" with an offer to settle for less than the amount they claim you owe.

Now if your debt is big enough, some collection agencies will try to scare you with legal-looking letters. They may even send you copies of a few of your latest credit card statements, thinking that this will make you "cave in." Read this carefully: **if collectors respond to your request by sending you copies of credit card statements, you may be able to figure out on what date you were first late and never got caught up.** GOTCHA!

I want to make another important point here. If, you were building a house and ordered (15 yds) of concrete, when the driver delivers the concrete he gives you a copy of the load slip. Now, when you pay the bill, granted you get a statement of the total amount owed, BUT, you also get a copy of the actual invoices from each delivery. Now, when you buy something on a credit card, you sign the slip with your signature that you purchased something. When you get your credit card statement, you will NEVER see the actual sales slip or invoice. They simply send you the amount owed. They NEVER send you the invoice. So, without an invoice, how can you determine that actual amount of money owed?

Okay, Fred, you owe money but you don't have enough to pay it back. **Are you ready to address your credit situation?** Remember, by paying high interest rates you are allowing someone to simply take an extra hundred dollars out of your paycheck without you even knowing it. Get serious! This is your hard-earned money, and you need every penny for the family.

9. NEGOTIATING WITH CREDITORS..

Negotiate To Lower the Amount Owed

So let's get back to work and figure out how you are going to turn the tables, and squeeze an extra hundred from the bill collectors instead. How can you do it? Well, here's a story about Happy Henry, the good ole boy who has been selling your family appliances for many years. You never wanted to tell him that his repairs were shoddy, because he never bothered you about monthly payments when you were late.

Happy Henry recently decided to retire, and his son Les has taken over the business. Les Happy Henry wants to expand the business, and buy a new building. But when he gets into the files, he discovers that there are six hundred customers who have owed the old man $1,000 for a year or more.

All materials contained here-in are the property of the R.Sauger Company under US Copyright TX0005895316/203-12-16 or otherwise referred to as being available under the US Freedom of Information Act.

That is $600,000 that could help him buy the new building! Since his dad wasn't able to collect over the years, he hires a collection company, and six hundred families in his town now have a derogatory item on their credit reports.

He's embarrassed when he sees these friends and neighbors around town, but he doesn't know what else to do. But then a strange thing happened – maybe a magical cloud of common sense wafted over his store and the town. Suddenly the hundreds of families came to Les Happy and tell him that they want to settle their back debts. Would he accept $500 – half of the balance – on their accounts, and call it good? The local mailman, Stamp Goode, is leading the group of families. Stamp says, "Les Happy, we will each give you $100 now, then make payments of $50 for the next eight months to pay the remaining $400."

Now this young college-educated upstart puts on his thinking hat. At the beginning of the day he had *nothing*; but if he if he accepts their offer, he will have $60,000 in cash, and brand new receivables of $ 540,000. That would be enough to go the bank and buy that office building that he wants so badly.

But before Les can run down to the bank, Stamp tells him, "I want you to sign this "settlement agreement" so that everyone knows when and how much to pay you. First, you agree to settle for $500 from each family. Second, you agree that as long as they are making these payments on time, you will make an entry on their report that they are *paying as agreed*; when they make their final payment, you will make an entry saying that their account has *been paid satisfactorily*.

The more Les Happy thinks about the deal, the more he likes it. Instead of putting half of the families in his town in credit prison, he could instead stand in line at the local supermarket and pass out calendars to them as friends and valued customers. And, this is the only way that he can buy the office building.

Les happily signs the settlement agreement. In the end, six hundred families negotiated their bill down and didn't have to get more credit. Les Happy turned out to be their banker and best friend. The families eliminated a charged-off collection from their credit reports and replaced it with "paid as agreed" and "paid satisfactorily" reports. Many of them see their credit scores jump up almost 60 points.

Thanks to Stamp's common-sense plan, the townspeople can now go and refinance their home for lower payments, buy a car at common sense interest rates, qualify for better rates on their credit cards and last but not least, tell their automobile insurance broker that they are shopping for better rates because their credit scores have improved. Many of them find they are now saving over $300 dollars a month because they used knowledge.

This is just a light-hearted, "best case" scenario, but it shows how you can use what you are learning in this book to raise your credit score. **From this day forward, I want you to be aware of the power you have when you owe money. Remember – you can negotiate with creditors even if you don't have any money.**

All materials contained here-in are the property of the R.Sauger Company under US Copyright TX0005895316/203-12-16 or otherwise referred to as being available under the US Freedom of Information Act.

Try this. Get in touch with one of your creditors and simply say, "Now I have some money, and I would like to pay you but I can't." Then just shut up and watch how quickly they come back with "why not?" The answer is very simple. You tell this "reject from the Harvard school of common sense" that if you paid him money now and he enters it as a *"Paid Collection"*, it would actually *lower* your credit score. So why would you pay him? You might as well pay one of your other creditors who will enter exactly what you want him to say on your credit report. That usually gets their attention! Now you can negotiate to pay pennies on the dollar and remove negative entries from your credit report.

Negotiate To "Re-Age" or "Cure" Your Account

Now, these crooks may tell you that they can't negotiate. Believe me, I have heard every story in the book. I have seen Office Managers who say, "I couldn't possibly negotiate, because that would be breaking the law!" or collections agents who say, "You wouldn't want me to lie, would you?"

This is all hogwash. The US Congress has already put laws in place that authorize creditors to delete prior paying history. For example, if you get behind on a student loan from the government, you can rehabilitate that loan by making nine payments on time. After receiving those nine payments, the US Government will direct Sallie Mae to delete the entire prior payment history. You can get a clean slate. How about them apples, Charley Brown?

So when a collector tells you they can't negotiate, roll up your sleeves and bring on the "dawgs". Tell these self-appointed pillars of justice, *"Honey, if it's good enough for Uncle Sam, then it's good enough for me. So, either you delete the record, or you do not get a DIME. I will give my money to someone else."* Believe me, *this works*.

The Federal Financial Institutional Examination Council (FFEIC) has put into place a policy that allows credit card companies, or any other open-ended creditor, to delete the prior paying history from a credit report. WHAT? Yes, this is true. It is called "re-aging," or "curing" a credit card history.

Because this is not a *law*, they do not *have to* agree to re-age your account. But if you were an otherwise good customer who ran into some problems, many creditors will agree remove those late payments if that is what it takes to get money from you.

A word of caution: *if you have a habit of making late payments, you can forget this strategy.* Once you screw up, it virtually becomes impossible to get this gift. Hardly anyone has ever heard of this re-aging approach, and I have surprised and amazed many of my mortgage friends who personally have been hurt by today's credit mess. Being able to re-age your account is like finding that long lost goose that lays golden eggs. See Chapter 16, Cleaning Up Your Credit Report, to see if you might qualify for re-aging, and instructions for how to negotiate.

All materials contained here-in are the property of the R.Sauger Company under US Copyright TX0005895316/203-12-16 or otherwise referred to as being available under the US Freedom of Information Act.

Whether you apply this knowledge to your own personal life or you help someone in your family, you will be amazed how the use of money changes. Remember: your goal is to quit giving anyone that extra hundred bucks each month simply because you have poor credit.

Paying A Settled Amount

Never disclose where you work or bank to a creditor. If you are asked for this information, simply say "no comment." Why? Because if your settlement falls through, and the creditor gets a judgment against you, knowing where you bank or work will make it easy for them to collect the judgment against you.

Never pay your settlements with a personal check. This is very important, as it prevents other creditors from learning about your financial status and getting a hold of your bank account numbers. Always get a cashier's check or money order, and be sure to get them from the post office, or a different bank than your own bank.

Always keep a copy of your money order or cashier's check and put it in a safe place! Collection agencies keep notoriously bad records, and if there's ever a dispute, it's your word against theirs. If you say you paid and they said you didn't, there's no way to prove it unless you have the copy of the money order or cashier's check.

Let's say you negotiated a settlement with a creditor for less than you originally owed. But now someone else is suing you for the balance. You check with your bank, and find out that when the creditor deposited your check, they crossed out the memo that said "payment in full." Is this legal? It may be, so read the following information carefully. *Some collection agencies will agree to settle with you for far less than you owe and then turn around and hire another collection agency to collect the difference.*

In some states this is illegal. Once a creditor deposits or cashes a check for payment in full, she can't come after you for the balance later even if she crosses out the words "payment in full" or writes, "I don't agree" on the check. The states listed below have a law to protect you in the event that the creditor tries to collect more money after you pay the agreed-upon settlement amount.

Arkansas, Michigan, Texas, Colorado, Nebraska ,Utah, Connecticut, New Jersey, Vermont, Georgia, North Carolina, Virginia, Kansas, Oregon ,Washington, Louisiana, Pennsylvania, Wyoming and Maine

Other states have modified this rule. In these states, if a creditor cashes a check for "payment in full," the creditor can explicitly retain his right to sue you by writing *"under protest"* or *"without prejudice"* on the check with his endorsement. By writing those *exact words*, he can then come after you for the balance later.

All materials contained here-in are the property of the R.Sauger Company under US Copyright TX0005895316/203-12-16 or otherwise referred to as being available under the US Freedom of Information Act.

This is called restrictive endorsement. If he uses different words, such as "**without recourse.**" on the endorsement, or if he communicates with you separately, notifies you verbally or writes on the check that it is partial payment, he **cannot** sue you for the balance later.

The states in which this law is enforced include ,Alabama ,Minnesota, Ohio, Delaware, Missouri, Rhode Island, Massachusetts, New Hampshire, South Carolina and New York.

If you don't see your state listed here, the creditor could possibly make a restrictive endorsement when they cash your check, meaning they can either sue you themselves later, or sell the remainder of your account to another bill collector. To protect yourself, always make sure to get any negotiated settlement agreement with a creditor in writing.

Never forget how much power you have when you owe money. First, understand that the term "small claims" means what it says. Most of the cases that come to small claims court are settled, adjudicated or dismissed *with no attorneys (lawyers) involved*. Now, I know that hearing the word "attorney" can paralyze you in fear. Even though my stepson is an attorney, I have to admit that lawyers cannot escape the negative reputation they have earned as a group.

The fictional firm of "Dewey, Cheatem and Howe" represents how most people view the legal system. *(Say the name out loud quickly and you will get the joke.)* Trust me, I am not on a mission to insult attorneys. I just want you to take a candid look at small claims courts and learn what you can do to defend yourself.

Most small claims courts have simple rules that you must follow. The first thing to remember is that ***if you don't follow the rules, you will automatically lose.*** Now, most people get hyper when they find out someone is suing them. After all, it might involve going in front of a judge and explaining why you won't/can't pay your bills. Embarrassing? You bet your Aunt Tillie's girdle it's embarrassing.

Most people want to pay their bills, but because they lost their job, got a divorce, had health problems or some other reason, they just don't have any money. If you can't pay, does that make you a bad person? No. You just need a little help to squeeze out of this mess. If you are served a notice that someone is suing you, *read the summons carefully*. In most cases, the summons simply notifies you that you are being sued and you have a certain amount of days in which to notify the court with your answer and show up and tell your side of the story.

Don't get so worked up that you cannot sleep! After months of being hounded by that idiotic bill collector, you now you finally have a chance to talk to someone about your bill. Now make sure ask yourself a few questions before you charge off to the courtroom looking for a confrontation:

All materials contained here-in are the property of the R.Sauger Company under US Copyright TX0005895316/203-12-16 or otherwise referred to as being available under the US Freedom of Information Act.

1. Do you agree with the amount of money being sued for?
2. Have you gotten collection letters and simply ignored them?
3. Do you have any money to settle this lawsuit?
4. Would you be nervous when an attorney asks you some questions? In certain situations you might decide not to show up in court. In other situations, you may decide you simply *must* show up in court. Let's look at some different situations:
5. **Do you agree with the amount of money they claim you owe?** If you do not agree with the amount of money that you are being sued for, then by all means show up and demand that the plaintiff provide *total proof of the debt*. For now, don't just make the determination as to whether or not you owe the debt – you also need to validate the amount of the debt.
6. **Have you received collection letters but ignored them?** In Chapter 8 we talked about how to deal with nasty letters threatening legal action. Well, not responding to those letters prior to the lawsuit throws a different light on the subject. You really do not have any defense – unless you are totally prepared with an affirmative [strong] defense and a possible counter suit. You may want to consult with a lawyer to determine whether you have a strong defense.
7. **Do you have any money to negotiate with?** If you really owe the debt but you think that the other party might settle for less, go for it. When the plaintiff's attorney has to get up early and drive a couple of hundred miles to show up in court at 8:30 AM, he will be irate if he has to drive home without any "spoils" from the war.

10. SMALL CLAIMS COURTS..

Negotiating in Small Claims Court

When you first show up to small claims court, the clerk of the court directs you to a mediator who is not familiar with the case. He or she will take you into a little room and now the system starts to work. The mediator sets the tone, and will first ask each party if they're willing to settle.

The plaintiff's attorney is empowered to accept a settlement on behalf of their client, and in most cases he is highly motivated to walk away with any amount of money. After all, he got up early in the morning, gave up his coffee and breakfast with his wife, and had to drive a couple of hours to get to court by 8:30 AM. He would not be a happy camper if he has to leave with no settlement, and come back to court for a trial at a later date. His ego may be "bruised". If you know that he is open to settlement, and you have the resources to make an offer, it might be good for you to settle.

All materials contained here-in are the property of the R.Sauger Company under US Copyright TX0005895316/203-12-16 or otherwise referred to as being available under the US Freedom of Information Act.

The important thing here is to keep your cards close to the vest. *Never, under any circumstances, let anyone know if you are trying to buy a house, or refinance or buy a car.* This is a "silent" signal to the plaintiff's lawyer that he is free to go for your jugular vein. He will smell blood and try to get all of the money he can. A good approach is *to show up with a couple of your paycheck stubs, a couple of your car payment stubs, household bills,* etc. and look at the mediator and ask them something like, "how do you propose we come to some kind of a financial agreement based on my income and necessary living expenses?"

After reviewing your information, the mediator might look at the attorney and say, "I could see a settlement here of $50 per month, and maybe cut the total amount in half." In effect, the opposing lawyer has just been told by the court that there is not much chance for him get anything, and something is better than nothing. It would be very difficult for the plaintiff's attorney to seek a trial (move to the next step) simply because you offered a settlement instead of paying in full.

Now, the attorney is not *required* to take your settlement. But in the trial, the Judge will always ask them why they wouldn't accept the offer that was brokered by an impartial mediator, since a trial might result in a judgment but still no money. It will always look like kind of a revenge move by the lawyer. One last word on going to small claims court. Don't worry – it's natural to be nervous in court, especially when you are looking into the eyes of a trained "bulldog". Remember, you have more power than you think.

Well, the black-and-white car with the flashing red lights has come into the neighborhood. Who's going to jail now? Uh oh, it's pulling into our driveway! What are we going to tell the nosy neighbors?! You don't have money to pay your bills, you don't know anybody who knows how to handle a situation like this, and you don't want your family to find out, you're really in a desperate situation. I hate to tell you that it didn't have to go this far –but right now, when you're broke, have no job and don't know where to go. Getting hit with a lawsuit is the last thing that you need. Right?

Well, let's crawl into this old man's brain and find out what others in your situation have done over the years. If the sheriff serves you papers that say, " Greetings from XYZ Civil Court," you are being sued. This document tells you that *you are not under arrest* – but *you must file an answer to the court within twenty days* from the date that you are served these papers.

First things first: if you fail to provide an answer, a default judgment may be entered against you and all sums claimed as owed will be awarded to the plaintiff. In other words, you automatically lose if you do not file an answer. *You simply have to file your answer.* Your don't have to hire a Washington lawyer to answer the complaint – your answer can be very honest and simple, such as, *"I do not agree with the amount being claimed as owed."* That's it, unless you want to use your armchair lawyer (a.k.a. brother-in-law) and come up with some legal jargon such as "Defendant has certain rights" and blah, blah, blah.

All materials contained here-in are the property of the R.Sauger Company under US Copyright TX0005895316/203-12-16 or otherwise referred to as being available under the US Freedom of Information Act.

11. LAWSUITS AND JUDGMENTS..............................

Lawsuit Threats: They Must Read You Your Rights

Charlie, the truth of the matter is you are being sued. But don't panic! Go get a cold drink and pay attention here, because this first lesson could have an impact on you for the rest of your life. I want you to think back to those "shoot-em-up" police TV shows, where the cop pulls the bad guy out of the car and says to his partner, *"Read him his rights, Bill!"*

When the police put someone under arrest, the law requires them to first advise the person of their Fifth Amendment right not to say anything that will incriminate them. If the cop fails to do this, the case may be thrown out when it goes to court.

This is called the "Miranda Act". As we discussed in Chapter 8, when a bill collector contacts you by phone or by mail, they are required by federal law to first advise you of your "mini-Miranda" rights. Again, they must say this *exact* statement: *This is an attempt to collect a debt. You have thirty days from the date that you receive this notice to dispute any portion of the debt. If you fail to respond within those thirty days, this office can only **assume** that the debt is valid and can pursue legal means to collect.* This is a big deal. *If they fail to notify you of your rights using the exact language of the law, they are in violation of the federal Fair Debt Collection Practices Act.*

If they do not read you your mini-Miranda rights, how do you prove it? You need either *written* proof (a copy of their letter), or *recorded* proof (a recording of their phone call to you. If you are being harassed, and if they are not following this law, they have a problem, and can be fined $1,000. But this problem will surface only if you do something about it.

Will They Really Turn My Account Over to an Attorney?

I know of just one example where a woman was sued by a credit card company. We were surprised, because most lenders do not sue for under $1,000. But in this case they had hired a law firm to represent them because they had a large number of cases that were very similar.

When a creditor says they are going to turn your case over to his lawyers, let me assure you that they are bluffing – *most* companies do not pay attorneys to sit around and wait for accounts to go delinquent so they can begin lawsuits. Lawyers are expensive, and they charge by the hour! Most creditors are more likely to hire an outside collections agency to collect for them, because it is more effective than paying an attorney.

All materials contained here-in are the property of the R.Sauger Company under US Copyright TX0005895316/203-12-16 or otherwise referred to as being available under the US Freedom of Information Act.

Statute of Limitations

As I mentioned in Chapter 6, the statute of limitations (SOL) in your state determines how many years a creditor can legally collect before the debt is classified as **time-barred**. (See the Appendix for Statue of Limitations by state.) But once an account is time-barred, any attempt to collect can be construed as a *deceptive means of collections*. There are very few cases where a creditor has been sued for deceptive means of collections, because most people who receive notices from collectors just go ahead and pay out of fear.

If you know that your account is beyond the statute of limitations for your state, and you notify the collector that the account is time-barred, then it becomes illegal for them to continue to contact you. But that does not prevent them from taking the case to court. As I discussed in Chapter 10, **you must defend against any legal action**; failure to respond will result in a default judgment against you - for a debt that you legally do not have to pay.

And what is the one piece of information you need to determine whether your account is past the SOL? You must know the date on which it first became delinquent. See Chapter 6 for more on this.

Getting Your Case Thrown Out or Judgment Removed

Read this section over and over. I want you to memorize it, so that when you are talking to your brother-in-law about a lawsuit, you know exactly what you are talking about. When you travel down the highway, a state police officer can write you a citation in any part of the state. Why? Because that is his *jurisdiction*, the territory over which he has authority. Now, a county deputy sheriff can only write you a citation in the county in which he has jurisdiction. He has no authority outside of his own county.

When you come to the courthouse to defend yourself against a lawsuit, the judge does not have jurisdiction over the courthouse. The sergeant-at-arms has that jurisdiction. The judge has a different kind of jurisdiction – he or she has authority over the *case* that they are ruling on. **Did you know that of 85% of the all of the money judgments awarded in this country are VOID?**

I couldn't believe it when my son told me this fact, but I went out and researched it, and it's true. Much as a chair needs four legs to stand, your case needs to have four indices (or items) in order for the judge to have jurisdiction over it. The four indices – or legs of the chair – for any case are:

All materials contained here-in are the property of the R.Sauger Company under US Copyright TX0005895316/203-12-16 or otherwise referred to as being available under the US Freedom of Information Act

1. Copy of the complaint
2. Proof of service
3. Affidavit from the person that has knowledge of (the debt *at the time* it was incurred.
4. Original contract, or a certified copy of the contract

This is important: *If any of the four items above are missing from the case, the judge does not have jurisdiction* .So why are 85% of all judgments void?

1. **The affidavit is almost always missing.** In most cases, the person who was present when the contract or obligation was incurred (signed), is long gone, and cannot be found. The attorneys assume that because you do not have the money or the experience to protest the case, you will never notice that the affidavit is missing.
2. **The original contract – or a certified copy of that contract – is often missing as well.** Four years after you signed the contract, it's really tough for an attorney to dig up the contract, which was filed away somewhere long ago. Very interesting.

What does that mean for you? It means that if the judge awarded the plaintiff (creditor) a default judgment or a judgment against you, you have the right to come back later (without any time limit) and petition the court to **vacate the judgment** because it is *"void on its face."*

Should You Go To Court?

If you failed to show up in court, the plaintiff is automatically granted a default judgment. But you think either the affidavit or the original contract are missing, you can always come back later and petition the court to **vacate the judgment for lack of subject jurisdiction.** And don't worry, the judge won't be embarrassed, because he never even saw the case. If you didn't show up, the clerk of the court just stamped the folder DEFAULT sent it on its way.

Are you deciding whether or not you should show up for your court case? We talked about this a bit in Chapter 10. You are your own decision maker here, but here are some guidelines:

- If you think that you have sufficient proof to show the judge or mediator that you do not owe the debt, or that the amount claimed as owed is incorrect, go for it.
- If you have some money, and are prepared to negotiate, go for it. See Chapter 9 for more on how to negotiate.
- If you really don't have money at all, you may want to stay home and accept the default judgment. Let's say you go to court, and the mediator gets the plaintiff to agree to reduce the total amount owed, and you agree to make a payment to them every month. If you end up missing one monthly payment, you will go to court all over again, only this time you will definitely get a judgment.

All materials contained here-in are the property of the R.Sauger Company under US Copyright TX0005895316/203-12-16 or otherwise referred to as being available under the US Freedom of Information Act.

If you decide to go to court, be prepared! In civil cases, the plaintiff's attorney will probably ask you to answer a lot of questions. This can get very intimidating, but you will be fine if you use some common sense. One very important question to prepare for is when either the opposing lawyer or the Judge hands you a document and asks, "Is this your signature?" Be very careful. Even though the paper may indeed have your signature on it, your answer should be, "It looks like my signature." From a legal perspective, if the document is **not the original**, is **not notarized**, or is **not a certified copy of the original** document, it is only "hearsay evidence."

Yes, this is true! To repeat, if the paper they ask you to look at is not notarized, or is not a certified copy of the original, it is just a photocopy of the original, which is not admissible as evidence. You are also entitled to ask the court for permission to ask the plaintiff's lawyer to respond to *your* questions! These question and answer segments are referred to as "interrogatories". Here's an idea – why not ask the judge to have the plaintiff to answer exactly the same questions they are asking you? They are all generic questions, such as:

1. Can you tell me when I last used the account?
2. Are you the guarantor on the account?
3. What is the name of your bank?
4. Do you agree with the amount?

Now the game is on! What difference will asking questions make in your case? Well, they may not know the answers to the questions they are asking you. if you can get their lawyer to look confused or not be able to answer a question, then you weaken their position.

A Credit Card Contract Is *Not* Proof Of Debt

The landmark case of *Shepard vs. Brennan* set the bar for what is now commonly called *validation*. In this case Shepard, the plaintiff and creditor, sued Brennan for a debt. Shepard's attorney presented a copy of the original "terms of the credit card agreement" as proof of the debt, but the Judge ruled that this was not sufficient evidence. The judge said that when the credit card agreement was signed (at the time the account was first opened), the agreement was based on *future debt* (all future charges.) The terms and conditions did not prove any of the charges or payments made by Brennan after the account was opened, and were therefore ruled inadmissible as evidence.

This is very important, because collection attorneys frequently present as *proof of the debt* a copy of the "terms of the agreement", which is only *proof of the contract*.

All materials contained here-in are the property of the R.Sauger Company under US Copyright TX0005895316/203-12-16 or otherwise referred to as being available under the US Freedom of Information Act.

12. FORECLOSURES..

Home Equity Loans And Adjustable Rate Mortgages

So you finally bought your dream home. What a deal! The salesperson at the homebuilder who sold it to assured you that the house would go up in value overnight. He said, *"If you sign the contract today, you're going to save thousands of dollars, because the price of the house is going up after Monday's sales meeting".* You bought the home on Friday and couldn't wait to tell your friends how smart you were.

The "Gold Rush" was on. Many thousands of folks just like you purchased homes in the belief that they would increase in value. Everyone was in "fat city," and there was no end in sight. If somebody had told you and your neighbors that home prices would crash in the near future, he would have been run out of town and hung from the highest limb. Everyone believed that home prices were going to keep rising, and the sky was the limit.

So what were you going to do with this new-found equity in your home? After all, you only paid $195,000 and now an identical home down the street is selling for $275,000. On paper, that's a profit of $80,000! Don't look now, but here comes the aggressive marketing guy from the local mortgage broker, and he says, "why don't you let me refinance your home so you can get that cash out now, and do what you want with it?"

The wheels in your head started turning. Now you could get rid of that ten year old rusty pick-up truck and come back from the local dealer with a brand spanking new F-150 – or maybe even one of those fancy Hemi V-8 engines. And the wife always did want a wide-screen TV! Now you had the chance to get those things that you deserved. And the marketing genius assures you that if you pay for the TV and truck out of your refinance proceeds, you can write off the interest on those things as mortgage interest. This was a perfect scenario, because of course your house would continue to go up in value. But was it too good to be true?

Let's take a look at that refinancing. The mortgage company offered you a (95%) loan based on the appraised value of your home. Now with an appraisal of $275,000 and a new principal balance of $261,250, you get *cash in hand* of $66,250. You are in la-la land. You never earned that much in a single year!

With just a stroke of the pen, you became a "genius." You *deserved* that new truck and the big wide-screen TV. Let's go into the details of this transaction. You were told that the payments would be low for the first couple of years and that they would adjust upward as the increase in interest rates would kick in. That didn't bother you because you were going to make more money or sell the house. This new loan was called an "***adjustable arm loan***", or maybe a "negative amortization loan". These loans are really tricky but they created a lot of money immediately for young couples.

All materials contained here-in are the property of the R.Sauger Company under US Copyright TX0005895316/203-12-16 or otherwise referred to as being available under the US Freedom of Information Act.

Let's say that the interest rate on your loan of $275,000 was 6%. With an adjustable loan, they would do is only charge you 3% for the first year and then
4% for the second year.

This simply meant that in the first year you were 3% short, and owed the lender that amount of difference. So, let's do some figuring. At 6%, the interest on $275,000 would be $16,500 in the first year. But because you only paid only 3% interest, or $8,250.00, you were able to cut your interest payments in half. Where did the other half go to? Well, you still owe the lender the difference between 3% and 6% -- the remaining $8,250 will be recovered by the lender later on.

But you weren't worried – after all, if the house was going up in value each year, your risk was minimized by the value of the home. WOW! Here you were living in a $275,000 home and making interest-only payments of $687 a month. Hell, that was less than paying rent in a two-bedroom apartment. Got the picture yet?

Facing Foreclosure

Now let's fast forward two years. You got used to paying only $687 a month, but now those back interest payments that you did not pay earlier are coming back to haunt you. All of a sudden your new payments jump up to over $2,000 a month. You cannot make that kind of a payment! You drive home in your pickup truck and watch some shows on your wide-screen TV, but nothing makes you feel better. Looks like you're headed for foreclosure.

I think it's a shame that there is no education available for new homeowners. While the market was booming, everyone thought they did not need advice. After all, they just made a cool $80,000 profit on their new home – how could anyone teach them anything? They knew it all. Every day, there are thousands of people in the United States who are going through foreclosure.

When you find yourself unable to make your house payments, you call the bank to try to work things out. But you find yourself talking to the village idiot, who does not care two hoots about you or your family. Your friendly banker has become a snarling tiger, and is mad as hell because you are not paying him. The phones start ringing off of the hook and your blissful home life has now become a living hell. You and your wife start to get into arguments, blaming each other for the mess you're in.

Did You Refinance?

STOP! Before you ready any further, answer this question: *Have you refinanced your primary home within the last three years?*

All materials contained here-in are the property of the R.Sauger Company under US Copyright TX0005895316/203-12-16 or otherwise referred to as being available under the US Freedom of Information Act.

1. If the answer is **YES**, then go directly to Page 70 and read more about the Truth In Lending Act (TILA.) Do not get confused with any other information in this chapter on Foreclosure.
2. If the answer is **NO**, then keep reading. **Defense Against Foreclosure** First of all, you are going to have to make some tough decisions, and it's important to not be influenced by your emotions. Many folks who are facing foreclosure simply pack up and walk away from their home in despair, because they don't have the knowledge or the resources to defend their rights.
3. I'm here to tell you that *you can walk away from your house, but the problem will not go away.*

Stop Payments Now

If you are in a situation where your home is going to be sold at a foreclosure sale (or you plan to sign a deed in lieu of foreclosure before the sale), you may choose not to make any more mortgage payments. You can put those monthly payments into a transition fund for your family. Just think about this. I know of many folks who have decided to stop making their mortgage payments because they cannot afford them. Let's say your house payment is $1,500 a month, and with legal help you are able to push out the your date of foreclosure for one year. At the end of the year, you will have saved $18,000. That, my friends is the equivalent of a 10% return on an $180,000 investment. The difference is that you got the profits from that investment without putting up one thin dime.

Bankruptcy Is Not An Easy Answer

What about bankruptcy? Despite whatever you hear from some "smooth tongued" attorney, *bankruptcy alone will not discharge your mortgage debt.* Bankruptcy will not make the debt go away – it only delays your payment of it.

If You Are Being Sued

Well, now the "pistols" are loaded, and you need to pay attention. When you receive papers from a process server, you are required to appear in court within twenty days from that date. Read the papers very carefully. **Do not let twenty days elapse without answering the complaint!** If you fail to answer the complaint, the party that is suing you will win a default judgment.

I have been preaching and teaching about credit for the last ten years, and this is serious. In Florida, *once you have a default judgment on your public records, it remains there for twenty years*. They are seven year terms, with an automatic renewal and then another renewal. Now Charlie, just try and buy a home in the future with that judgment hanging over your head!

All materials contained here-in are the property of the R.Sauger Company under US Copyright TX0005895316/203-12-16 or otherwise referred to as being available under the US Freedom of Information Act.

You may be nervous and scared of the Judge and the Attorneys, but think about it! With such steep consequences, why not show up in court to defend yourself? Keep reading, and discover some of the best reasons to fight.

Beware of Foreclosure Saviors!

These days, a new breed of financial shark has entered the scene – let's call him a "foreclosure savior." He sits you down, and in a very solemn tone he tells you that he is someone who will save you. You will lose your home, of course, but at least you will end up with sufficient cash to be able to relocate and find a new place to live. And this savior might even have a home of lesser in value in mind. Out of the goodness of his heart, he will rent it to you on a lease-to-own option, and you can buy it once you get back on your feet.

It all sounds good, doesn't it? You say yes, and this "thing" of a human being now gets started. He has you sign your deed over to him *in lieu of foreclosure,* so that the lender has to deal with him instead of you. He will make your mortgage payments for you and negotiate to buy the house from the bank on a *short sale.* What's in it for the shark? When he buys your home on short sale, he will pay an amount that is less than what you owed on it, plus any maintenance or repair work that has to be done. And believe me, once this shark gets his hands on your home, he will make *sure* that there is a lot of work to be done on it! He will take lots of pictures of your home, showing it in disrepair and surrounded by weeds, and send them to the bank's agent.

This agent is called a *loss mitigator*, .and he is the one who tells the bank whether or not to accept the shark's offer. Let's say you owe $260,000 on the home, and the shark offers the bank just $150,000. The bank will sometimes take the offer just because they do not want to own real estate. Your house is simply a non-performing asset on their books – how do they explain that to their investors?

Another reason the bank may accept the offer is to cut their losses as all homes in your neighborhood drop in value. Think about it – since you moved out, the grass has not been cut and it looks terrible. The economy is in the tank, so there are no new homes being sold and builders in the neighborhood are shutting down their models. Your house is probably not the only one in the neighborhood that is going as a short sale! The only sales that an appraiser can relate to are other so-called "short sales", so the values of all of the homes in your area drop. By the time the loss mitigator sees your house, there is a good chance that he will tell the lender take the shark's deal.

The Bank May Not Own Your Home

What do I mean, the bank might not own your home? How in the world can I say that? Well, pay attention – I want you to read this section over and over until you understand it. Remember when you closed on the mortgage? You signed two significant documents:

All materials contained here-in are the property of the R.Sauger Company under US Copyright TX0005895316/203-12-16 or otherwise referred to as being available under the US Freedom of Information Act.

1. One was the *property deed* that was recorded with the county.

2. The other (and more important) document was the *mortgage note*.

This is the piece of paper that you signed that promised to make loan payments to someone for thirty years, or whatever the term was. When the process server came to your house to serve you foreclosure papers, you probably got very nervous, and hid the papers so the kids couldn't see them, and neither could your friend when she came over for coffee. **But if you look closely at those papers, there are some clues that may tell you that the bank most probably does not own your home.**

If the lawyer for the bank is asking the court to accept something called a *lost note affidavit,* that means they cannot find your original promise to pay (the mortgage note.) That means they really don't own the home, and would be trespassing. They are asking the court to allow them throw you and your family out on the street, when they don't have any legal interest in the proceedings.

I ask you, would you let a total stranger bully you into leaving the home that you worked so hard to buy? I know the answer to that one. Hell, you would have hit him on the head with a frying pan just for bothering you! But because the stranger is someone with an official badge, and because the papers came from a court, you were afraid and didn't think anyone could help you. *Let's go back to the "foreclosure help" scams.* Maybe you and your husband became got bad advice; maybe you even paid money to a shark and got nothing.

Here is where we tie in the short sale scam: *if your bank did not own the home, then how could they sell it to someone on a short sale?* Did you ever wonder why it takes so long to get approval of a short sale? It's because the bank doesn't own the home, and they must get approval from a judge to approve the lost affidavit motion before they can make the sale. In most cases the consumer is not represented in court, and there is no objection to the lost affidavit motion.

OK, all of this is enough to confuse a Philadelphia lawyer. In street talk, this means that the company that you thought you were getting the money from was just a beginning of a very large scheme on Wall Street that is intended to confuse you.

Confused? Hell, even after I have read this material over and over, I am still trying to figure it out. Here is what I can say: *it is likely that the mortgage note you signed – and it must be the original – has either been purposely put someplace where only certain people know where it is, or it has been lost.*

When you sat down at closing after the nerve-wracking run-up to this moment, you experienced it as a success, the culmination of a lot of effort to prove you were a credit-worthy client deserving of a loan to purchase a home or property, the biggest investment most of us ever make.

All materials contained here-in are the property of the R.Sauger Company under US Copyright TX0005895316/203-12-16 or otherwise referred to as being available under the US Freedom of Information Act.

You probably had no clue that the documents placed in front of you could be deceptive – but they were. They were *very* deceptive. ***This might be one of the most potent financial weapons you have to save your home.*** So for God's sake, read this section again and again! If you don't understand it, have your wife or your brother-in-law read it to you. It would take another book just to give you the basics of what a Truth In Lending Act (TILA) Audit is. But this section provides some of the basic information, and maybe, just maybe, you are eligible for this action. First, *you must have re-financed within the last three years,* and once you uncover TILA violations, you will need legal representation in court. The journey is long, but the rewards are great. You can get all of your costs back, plus your attorneys fees and triple damages.

13. FORECLOSURE, REFINANCING & TILA VIOLATIONS.........

Canceling Your Mortgage

You have the right to rescind or cancel a mortgage only if:

1) you have refinanced this home as your primary residence within the last three years, and
2) you have performed a ***Truth In Lending Act (TILA) Audit*** and found that material errors were made at the original application for, or closing of, the mortgage.

When these conditions are met, you have **three years from the date of the closing** to notify the lender that as a result of a TILA Audit you are submitting your letter of rescission. By the time you are reading this book, you may already be close to this deadline. I highly recommend that you talk to an attorney who is familiar with foreclosure laws as soon as possible.

TILA Audit

If you meet these conditions, your first step will be to locate a qualified forensic audit company or individual in your area. There should be no cost to get a preliminary review of your mortgage/closing documents. Once the professional reviews your documents, they will also let you know if you qualify, and if so, how many violations were found and what money damages may be available to you.

While then the cost of the audit varies, I have seen them run as high as $1,500. My office, R. Sauger Company www.mycreditprofessor.com) currently charges $995 for a TILA Audit. The initial fee takes care of the administrative phase of the process. If litigation is necessary, you will need to make a separate agreement with the attorney, and additional attorney fees will be required. Most attorneys require a small upfront cost for filing, but base their final fee on a percentage of the award.

All materials contained here-in are the property of the R.Sauger Company under US Copyright TX0005895316/203-12-16 or otherwise referred to as being available under the US Freedom of Information Act.

That is entirely between you and the attorney. *The process should not damage your credit rating.* If you are current in your payments, your credit report should reflect two things – that the mortgage debt was satisfied in full, and that it was satisfied early. If, on the other hand, the payments are in arrears, then the lender will often report this to the credit bureaus. Once you receive the Judge's order, you can have the negative item removed from your credit report. Why? Because the courts have ruled that the lender is NOT the owner of the note or the holder in due course, and therefore cannot be a furnisher of information to the Credit Reporting Agencies. *(If anyone could furnish information about you to CRAs, then anyone could report anything about anybody. That would be havoc in our system.)*

You can also utilize "injunctive relief". Simply said, this means that if your credit has taken a hit from any type of action and the situation has been solved, paid or settled; but you have no way of getting it off of your credit report, you can do the following. Petition the court for injunctive relief to remove the derogatory entry from your credit report. The Judge grants the motion and now the credit bureaus, who were not aware of your action, must now removed the item or be in contempt of court. Very interesting.

If you are behind on your payments, you can still go though the TILA Audit process, but It is better if you are not. *The lenders and courts are more likely to favor your requests if you start the process with "clean hands" and are current in your payments.* Here are some important things to know about a TILA Audit:

1. In most cases a TILA mortgage debt resolution process takes three to six months. If filing a suit is required, the process could take up to two years.

2. If you have one or more bank accounts with this lender, you should move them before beginning any debt resolution process. Do this without delay, as the bank may freeze your accounts.

3. You can only use the TILA Audit process on your *primary* residence.

4. This process will not work on private loans. A private loan is one in which any person or business (not a mortgage company) loans you the money and the two of you have agreement on when and how to pay. These types of private loans are not regulated by the Real Estate Settlement Procedures Act.

5. Remember that the bank or mortgage company will not be harmed by this process! They borrowed against your promise to repay the note, essentially creating money out of thin air. They did not put out any money out of pocket.

6. If the lender tries to contact you, do not under any circumstances respond either on the phone or in writing. Simply forward the name or letter to your attorney, and they will take care of it.

All materials contained here-in are the property of the R.Sauger Company under US Copyright TX0005895316/203-12-16 or otherwise referred to as being available under the US Freedom of Information Act.

Rescission

Do you ever wish you could go back in a time machine and take your mortgage back? Well, in certain situations you may be able to do just that. **Rescission** is the act of "rescinding", or reversing, a transaction. It essentially unmakes a contract between the parties. The Truth in Lending Act (TILA) provides for rescission rights, as does common law, and many states' Deceptive Business Practice Acts.

Ordinarily, a rescission involves giving back everything you received in exchange for getting back everything you gave. In a mortgage situation, it means **the right to get back all of the interest, points, closing costs, attorney fees and other costs that you incurred at or after closing as a result of the transaction.** Rescission does not mean the borrower doesn't owe any money at all to the lender. In today's business environment, I have not seen any cases where the lender fought a rescission all the way through a trial. Everyone that we have heard of has been settled without litigation.

The reason that lenders want to settle without litigation is that a TILA violation shows on the lender's credit risk assessment, which is reviewed when the lender goes to the Federal Reserve to get money. A lender with a record of TILA violations will be charged a higher rate than a bank with a clean record. *What rescission does mean is that the mortgage lien is extinguished and so is the note.* Why is this important? Because it converts a secured debt, non-dischargeable in bankruptcy to an unsecured debt, which is wholly dischargeable in bankruptcy.

After the lender admits to the rescission – or it is decreed by the courts – the total deficiency amount is then reduced by the refunds of points, interest, and closing costs paid, plus damages and attorney fees suffered as a result of the issues raised in this these material violations. And here is the icing on the cake: unless the party coming into court or the auction as a representative of the lender can prove that they have received their instructions and authorization from *a party who is authorized to give those instructions,* then they lack authorization, they lack legal standing and *they are probably committing a fraud on the borrower, the court and everyone else.* There are rarely any damages involved, but your case may be dismissed "with prejudice," which bars the plaintiff from taking you back to court on the same issue.

Quiet Title

Who really owns the title to your home? Remember, the basket of mortgage notes from Chapter 5? *When your loan was assigned, sold and transferred multiple times, broken up into thousands of pieces, and intermingled with many others in the portfolio, sometimes with cross guarantees from one portfolio to another, the lender committed a foreclosure offense.* This process probably started before your first payment was due on the mortgage loan and long before you came to know the real facts of the loan withheld from him in these secret devious practices. You, the borrower, are a victim of fraud.

All materials contained here-in are the property of the R.Sauger Company under US Copyright TX0005895316/203-12-16 or otherwise referred to as being available under the US Freedom of Information Act.

Because of this fraud, you are able to pursue *a quiet title foreclosure*, which is the reverse of a traditional foreclosure. That's right - instead of the lender foreclosing on you, you foreclose on them! Why? Because, the true owner was never disclosed to the borrower. Just think about that for a minute. *When you closed on your mortgage, you were never told who was going to own the note.* **By depriving you of this information, it would be impossible for you to send a rescission notice to anyone.** This was a violation of your legal rights.

By performing a TILA Audit you may determine there could be thousands of entities or owners, none of whom have been disclosed to you, the borrower, despite attempts to secure this information. By pursuing a quiet title action, you sue "John Doe," identified as all persons having an ownership interest in the mortgage lien on the property in question.

This action states that you have been notified of a transaction, but you have not been advised of what entities or people own this interest. And since this is a violation of the Truth In Lending Act, you wish to rescind (void) the original mortgage.

In Ohio and other states, the inability of the lender or mortgage servicer to produce the original note and mortgage, combined with their inability to produce the documentation regarding the assignment or sale of the loan has resulted in *de-linking the mortgage from the security interest in the home* and the cancellation of the note – **giving the borrower (you) free and clear title to the property that was subject to the original loan transaction.**

If the court demands that the mortgage servicing company be named as nominal Defendant or Respondent, the mortgage servicing company has only one job: to produce information and proof of ownership of the loan. It is doubtful that anyone, least of all the mortgage servicing entity will be able to fulfill this condition.

Thus a default judgment will be entered against the lender, and then you stop paying the mortgage.

You now have a recorded judgment relieving your property of any mortgage lien, and offsetting the note with the refunds and damages payable to the victim – *thus satisfying the entire principal of the note and awarding attorney fees to the victim/petitioner.*

What Is the Difference Between Quiet Title and Rescission?

These are two very separate issues. Quiet title deals with the *ownership of the home*. In a quiet title action you are putting the lenders' toes to the fire for not revealing to you who the other owners are. Most quiet title actions will refer to "un-named parties." On the other hand, a rescission action deals with ownership of the note. Because they did not reveal the many parties who owned your mortgage note, the lender is in violation of the Truth in Lending Act. You can legally "reverse" the mortgage agreement, and recoup all transaction costs incurred.

All materials contained here-in are the property of the R.Sauger Company under US Copyright TX0005895316/203-12-16 or otherwise referred to as being available under the US Freedom of Information Act.

Look On The Bright Side

So what have you learned about foreclosure? I hope you can see that the equity that you had in your home is gone. Some of your lucky friends sold their homes at a high price and made huge profits. I suspect that you may be emotional at the prospect of losing the first home you ever owned. That is normal, and you shouldn't feel ashamed.

Let's look back at how much cash you really put into the deal. How much did you receive in tax refunds because you deducted the mortgage interest from your tax returns? Add this all up, and maybe it is not as bad as you think. Let's say that between you and your wife, your combined income was $50,000. If you took simple deductions, you would pay tax on about $35,000. So at 20%, your tax bill was $7,000. If you did not have that much deducted from your paycheck you owed the IRS some money.

Let's also say that you bought a home for $200,000 and put nothing down. Since you were able to deduct the interest from your tax returns, you made a very good investment. For example, a $200,000 loan at 7% means $14,000 in interest payments. Now you have $35,000 minus $14,000 in interest which gives you adjusted taxable income on $21,000. At 20%, your tax bill would be $4,200.

You saved $2,800 on your taxes, and that is cash in your pocket. That, my friends, is the equivalent of earning a 10% return on a $28,000 investment. But remember – you didn't have to put the cash down. So your tax savings was very good thing.

14. AUTO REPOSSESSIONS………………………………..

Was Your Car Sold In A Commercially Responsible Manner?

I'll bet that you have a friend or family member who has gone through a repossession and didn't have a clue what to do. I have helped over one hundred and sixty families with repossessions to purchase a home, simply by helping them learn how to use the law in their favor.

Following are two methods that may help you either reduce the amount of the deficiency on your credit report, or delete the derogatory item altogether. Years ago, I came across an eye-opening Florida Repossession case that I just couldn't put down. I stayed up until 3:30 AM reading this case, and eventually my wife finally gave up hollering at me and just went to sleep. In this Tallahassee, FL case, the Barnett Recovery Corp (Barnett Bank) was attempting to sue a Mr. Johannesson for a deficiency on a repossession of his pickup truck.

All materials contained here-in are the property of the R.Sauger Company under US Copyright TX0005895316/203-12-16 or otherwise referred to as being available under the US Freedom of Information Act.

(The deficiency was the amount of money claimed as still owed on the note after the vehicle was sold.) Mr. Johannesson's case was in the 6th Circuit Court of the State of Florida, on June 4, 1996. In this case, the judge ruled that because the vehicle was sold at a "dealer only auction," to which the public was not invited, the amount received at the auction constituted full value and therefore the bill was **paid in full.**

No wonder I couldn't put it down – this was powerful stuff! The Judge said that because this vehicle was sold in a commercially unreasonable manner, the amount of the sale or funds received denied the bank from getting a deficiency judgment. The vehicle debt would now appear on Mr. Johannesson's credit report as paid in full.

A few years later, a deputy from the local Sheriff's department in Florida came to me for help in getting approved for a mortgage. While the deputy and his wife had gone through bankruptcy a few years earlier, they had kept their credit spotless since then. When his wife needed a car to get to work, he stopped at one of the local used car dealers and bought her a car. She drove it for just two weeks before the transmission conked out.

When the irate deputy took the car back to the dealership and said "fix it," they said sorry, "you own it". Unable to come to an agreement, the deputy said, "I will leave the car here until it is fixed."

Guess what? A couple of months later, he got a notice from an attorney in Ohio who represented the bank that financed the car. The notice said that the car had been sold at auction, and he must now pay them the $5,700 delinquency (difference) within ten days or they would seek legal action to have his paycheck garnished.

This poor guy was shaking. After all, a deputy with a garnishment doesn't look too good. We asked him if the bank had sent him a notice notifying him as to when and where the vehicle was going to be sold. The deputy produced the document and sure enough, the bank had notified of the auction location. We told him to take his wife down to this auction place to see if he could buy a car. And we told him to bring his digital camera and take pictures of the entrance. The deputy came back in a couple of hours and showed us the pictures. Sure enough, the sign said *"Dealers Only – Public Not Allowed"*.

We sat down with him and helped him draft a letter to the attorney in Ohio. In his letter, the deputy simply said: "I am confused about this problem and therefore I am going to ask a Judge to sort it out in my county of Lee, Florida. It appears as though you might be attempting to collect on a debt that might not legally exist. Enclosed is a copy of Florida Case Law wherein the lender was deprived of a deficiency judgment because the vehicle was sold at a 'Dealers Only Auction.'

All materials contained here-in are the property of the R.Sauger Company under US Copyright TX0005895316/203-12-16 or otherwise referred to as being available under the US Freedom of Information Act.

Enclosed is a copy of the, entrance which clearly shows signage that prohibits the public from entrance. We also enclosed a copy of Florida Case Law regarding this issue. Some folks might interpret this action as possible extortion as there clearly is no debt. Now, because you have used the US Mail over state lines, is this a violation of the RICO Act? We of course do not understand the complexities of these things. Therefore we await your response prior to our submitting this for adjudication."

It was sent *by certified mail* with *a return receipt*. Well, the deputy came into my office in a couple of days with an envelope and said "Mr. Sauger, I just got this letter from the attorney in Ohio. Are they going to garnish my wages?" We opened the envelope together. In the letter, the Ohio attorney told the deputy that the case was closed, *he owed no money,* and that they were notifying all credit bureaus to *delete the account.*

While each state has its own laws on repossession, most require that the creditor/lien holder sell your vehicle in a "commercially responsible manner", and that they notify you in writing as to where and when your vehicle is going to be sold. If the vehicle is sold at a Dealers Only sale, which is not open to the public, the auto will probably sell at a below-market price, which is *possible extortion*. And if any of the attempts to collect using the US Mail crossed state lines, then this could also be a violation of Racketeer Influenced and Corrupt Organizations (RICO) Act, the same federal law that is used to prosecute the mafia.

One time, when I was teaching a class in Naples, Florida, a young man named Richard got up and left the class without warning. I later found out that after reading the workbook's chapter on repossessions a few times, he was inspired to action. He had sent letters to Transunion and Equifax asking about the auto repossession that was on his report. The next day he got a certified letter with a judgment for $4,876.92.

Richard took matters into his own hands and drove down to Ugly Duckling Auto Sales, the company that had repossessed his car. He marched into the manager's office and demanded to know where and when his vehicle had been sold. They tried to throw him out, but Richard was hell-bent on getting the truth. In his own words,

*"I went down there with my credit report and my workbook and they did not want to talk. So I asked one more time **where and when**. They told me they sold it back to the dealer for $500. WHAT?! I let them look at the FL law on repos and I walked out **paid in full**. They said it would be off my report in 48 hours. Regis, you are the main man. The class paid for itself, a hundred times over."*

– Richard Harsh

All materials contained here-in are the property of the R.Sauger Company under US Copyright TX0005895316/203-12-16 or otherwise referred to as being available under the US Freedom of Information Act.

I have lots of stories about how average folks have been victimized by the system. Are the dealers so cruel that they would knowingly hurt someone's credit by listing a repossession when they have not complied with the laws? I don't know that answer, but I do know this: if you have been the victim of an incorrect or illegal repossession, with a little determination you can get your credit back on track. Just remember, your name is on the title as the OWNER and the lender is on the title as a lien-holder. You legally own the vehicle until the auctioneer says "SOLD" What, IF the vehicle brought more than what is owed? Did you get a check?

Was Your Car Damaged or Stripped on its Way to Auction?

Here is another sweet little tidbit about repossessions. When that repo man hooks onto your car in the middle of the night, he inventories the contents and reports the physical condition of the car. Why? Because, his company is liable for any damage or theft of your possessions while they have the vehicle in their possession. Let's say that there was a top-of-the-line $10,000 stereo system in your car, which was repossessed and put up for auction. The vehicle was worth $20,000 with the stereo system intact, and you owe $15,000 on the auto loan. If the car had sold for that amount, you could potentially have gotten a check for $5,000.

But what if your car shows up at the auction place with the stereo mysteriously gone? Without the stereo, the car might only sell for $10,000. When the auctioneer shouts "Sold!" you now owe the bank $5,000. If you cannot pay this amount within a certain period of time, you will get a judgment of that amount on your credit report.

Who stole the "boom box?" (It's kind of like that old song "who stole the *kieshka?*") You will probably never find out. It's not your fault that the stereo was stolen, but because you are broke, you cannot hire a lawyer. And even if you did, most lawyers do not want to take these cases without a retainer, because there's not much to win. But now that you're reading this book, and you are still "mad as hell" because you thought your car was worth more, what do you do? Well, *you start with your legal right to view all of the documents and elements relating to the sale.*

When the wrecker driver tows the car to the storage area, he signs a **condition report** that his company furnishes to the insurance company and/or the lien holder. You have a right to view the condition reports that the wrecker driver, the storage yard and the auto auction receiving area generate. So you obtain these reports, and lo and behold, the storage yard condition report shows your vehicle with a $10,000 stereo system. But the auto auction report shows that *there was no stereo equipment in the car when it arrived at the auction place.*

Who stole the stereo? From the reports, it appears that the auto transporter either stole it, had a friend swipe it, or someone saw the stereo while he was having his lunch at the local "greasy spoon" and swiped it from the car. No matter what happened, **the insurance company used by the transporter is legally responsible for that condition of the car while it is in transport.**

All materials contained here-in are the property of the R.Sauger Company under US Copyright TX0005895316/203- 12-16 or otherwise referred to as being available under the US Freedom of Information Act.

Now, this kind of stuff goes on every day. How can you get the straight answers and eliminate this repo horror story from your life? Believe me, none of the players want to step up to the plate and take the heat for your missing stereo. But *if you are persistent and get all of the "who, where, and when" information from the condition reports of your repossessed vehicle, you most probably can win a lawsuit against all of the parties involved in the act of repossessing your vehicle.*

So get acquainted with your state laws and your rights under repossession! Without your knowing this, you might be getting a deficiency judgment for $5,000 instead of a check for $5,000. No one, and I say it emphatically, **no one ever goes to the trouble of getting all of their repossession paperwork**. But ask yourself, *"Can I afford to just give some stranger money simply because, he is in a power position and I am broke and do not know the laws?"*

Would you give me money if I just show up at your house on payday and demand it? Of course not. That's incredibly stupid, especially when the knowledge you need to win is available. Before I close this chapter on repos, I want to ask you a question. *When does the seven-year period of reporting derogatory credit begin?* You may get offended by an old man who keeps asking the same question! But I say so what, at least you will soon know more about your credit reports than anyone else walking the streets.

15. MEDICAL BILLS AND HIPPA..........................

How HIPAA Can Affect Your Medical Debts

Although most people think they are the same thing, there is a big difference between your medical records and your medical bill. There is a federal law called the Health Insurance Portability and Accountability Act (HIPAA) that gives you the power to limit who can see your medical records. Although your immediate physician can see your records, a bill collector cannot look at them *unless you authorize it in writing*.

When you went to the dentist or doctor office, they probably had you sign a release form that allows them to place your account into collections if you fail to pay your bill. But remember this: the wording in this release is for your medical *billing*, not your medical *records*. Why is this important? **Because doctors and hospitals routinely overcharge their patients** -- not by intent, but by habit.

They are notorious for making paper errors and having bad writing. Here's an example. Let's say that at 7:30 AM, the doctor comes into your hospital room and says, "Sit up Charlie, I'm going to look you over and see if you can go home". So you sit up, he looks into your eyes, ears and nose. Beats you on the back a few times with a rubber hammer and says, "OK Charlie, you're out of here." At 8:00 he signs the chart and replaces it into that little metal clip folder at the end of your bed.

All materials contained here-in are the property of the R.Sauger Company under US Copyright TX0005895316/203-12-16 or otherwise referred to as being available under the US Freedom of Information Act.

Guess what he just did? He legally released you from the hospital and signed off as your Doctor, ending his responsibility to you unless he specifies a follow-up appointment. Now after the doctor leaves, you get up from your bed and kind of sneak over to the bathroom in your Christian Dior backless gown and reach for your clothes. But then a loud voice bellows out, "Where do you think you're going?" You turn around and see a nurse who looks like the starting guard for the New York Giants. You answer meekly, "I'm going home – the doctor just released me". But she says "get back into that bed and wait for the paperwork to come down". So back into bed you go.

Soon afterwards a "wee little lassie" with a cute ribbon in her hair and a big smile comes in and asks you what you want for lunch. You say you don't need lunch because you're going home. She insists that you order something *just in case* you are still there, so you ask for a ham and cheese. Your sandwich arrives at 11:30 with a small coke. You're a little hungry, so you eat the sandwich, still in your bed. Now the nurse returns and tells you get out of bed, get dressed and be on your way. On the way out, you notice that hospital checkout time was 11:00.

When you get your medical bill, it shows an additional day at a cost of $750. But remember, your medical records will indicate that the doctor discharged you at 8:00 AM, before the next billing day began. So, now you get the picture: *the extra day will show up on your medical bill, but not on your medical record*. That, my friend, is one expensive ham and cheese sandwich. Here is where it gets sticky. If you can't pay your bill and it goes to the collection agency, that $750 is included in the debt they are collecting. They naturally are on commission and want everything they can get.

Here's another example of how they can overcharge you. Let's say the doctor ordered 200 units of Sodium Penathol for you, but the pharmacy only had it in 600 unit containers. Your medical bill will show 600 units, but your medical records will only show the 200 units. Legally, the *hospital can only charge you for the amount of medicine your Doctor prescribed*. But, they get away with overcharging all of the time, because average folks don't know the difference.

How To Deal With Medical Collections

The most powerful strategy you have is to reduce the amount claimed as owed. It can be intimidating, but it is very important that you get all of the details. You have the power because **you are legally entitled to get a full copy of your medical records**. The business office might charge you a couple dollars per page for this, but having your records is invaluable when negotiating with collection agencies. You can have 100% accurate information when they only have a copy of the account. There is a major difference between the medical records and the billing records.

When a collection agency comes after you for money you owe on medical bills, you have every right to have those folks **prove the debt**. But how can they prove the debt without viewing your confidential medical records? There's the catch! They absolutely cannot prove the billing record without access to your medical record – and you can legally keep those records private under HIPAA laws.

All materials contained here-in are the property of the R.Sauger Company under US Copyright TX0005895316/203-12-16 or otherwise referred to as being available under the US Freedom of Information Act.

If there is no proof of debt, there is no debt. Nobody ever thinks about this strategy! Because very few people understand HIPAA laws, they are unable to defend themselves from collectors.

16. CLEANING UP YOUR CREDIT REPORT...............................

A Quick Lesson in What Your Credit Report Contains

Lace up your boots, strap yourself in and listen up. This is so powerful that I recommend that you really study this section a few times over to get a better understanding of "how to negotiate debts" and realize how much power you have when you owe money. The information contained in your credit file, or **credit report** is used to calculate your **credit score**. Your credit report will typically reflect the credit cards, car and home loans that you've taken on and paid off for many years.

There are no penalties for having used credit in the past, so long as the payments were made on time. If, however, there were late payments or charge-offs, *you'll need to take action to try to minimize these entries:*

1. If you have some money, you can negotiate with creditors to reduce the amount owed and/or remove negative entries. See Chapter 9 for more information.

2. If your position is that the payments were not late or that there were mitigating circumstances, you also have the option to add a short written consumer statement to your credit files.

3. If you find errors in your report – in the amount owed, the date of first delinquency, duplicate entries, etc. – then there are several ways to update or remove these entries.

Get Copies of Your Credit Reports

Under new Federal Law, you are entitled to see your credit report, at no charge, once a year. You can request your reports by phone, mail or online. The only site that I know of that does not charge for this service is www.annualcreditreport.com. I have found that the other sites that advertise free credit reports are packed with promotions to get you to buy into their marketing schemes. Be sure to read carefully before you agree to anything.

Because the three credit reporting agencies – TransUnion, Equifax and Experian – may have different information on file for you, you need to review all three reports carefully. At www.annualcreditreport.com, each agency will have a button to click, so be sure to click all three. Once into the site and you see an entry, look to the right and it will have another button that says "details". You must click "details" so that the box comes up showing the details of that entry. This will show your payment history, credit limits, charge-off dates and all of the other stuff you need to fully understand your credit report.

All materials contained here-in are the property of the R.Sauger Company under US Copyright TX0005895316/203-12-16 or otherwise referred to as being available under the US Freedom of Information Act.

Review Your Reports for Errors

Now that you have printed out your three reports, get your yellow highlighter and let's go to work. *Remember: over 80% of today's credit reports contain errors!*

1. First, check to see that your name is spelled correctly. This can be the basis for identity theft.

2. Highlight the columns on top that show the name of the "furnisher of information" Sometimes you will see the same account with different names or furnishers. This means that more than one company is either trying to collect or has purchased this account.

3. Also highlight the dates of opening, high credit, payment history, charge-off dates and balance due.

Look very carefully when you analyze each entry, and use a notebook to keep a list of the mistakes you have found.

Multiple Creditors For One Account

Sometimes, you will notice that an account on your credit report is being reported by more than one furnisher. This happens when an account is sold to a collector, and that collector gives up on collecting and resells it to another collector. This is not really such a big deal in itself, but it does cause errors in reporting. If you see multiple creditors for one account, simply go the validation of debt process. It is the original creditor that can be held liable for any violations of the Fair Debt Collection Practices Act.

It's also important to know that *the history of the account must follow the account*. For instance, if the account was first opened in January of 2003 and became delinquent in June of 2004, then that is the ONLY history that can go with the debt when it is sold. If any subsequent furnisher of information fails to follow this order, *they are guilty of providing false information on your credit report*. That is one window of opportunity that you have because most cannot find nor do not know when your account was first late.

(1) Send a letter to the credit bureau and ask them to *verify* the debt.

(2) Follow up with a letter to the furnisher of information asking them to *validate* the debt.

(3) Lastly, send a letter to the credit bureaus asking them to *remove* that item, because the debt could not be validated.

All materials contained here-in are the property of the R.Sauger Company under US Copyright TX0005895316/203-12-16 or otherwise referred to as being available under the US Freedom of Information Act.

Collection agencies frequently get caught aging an account by showing the date of opening of the account as the date that they either purchased or were assigned the account. See Chapter 7 for more on Aging Accounts.

Multiple Account Numbers for One Account

Sometimes you will see multiple account numbers for one account, which can be very confusing. Each company assigns their own number to an account, and in a lot of cases they report their own account number to the credit bureaus. *This is not accurate reporting.*

When you ask a creditor or collector to verify the information on your account as accurate, you should always use the account number that you have. Do not use their account number – it is what they do to confuse you. Remember whose side the credit reporting agencies are on! *You are the one with poor credit, and since they get 24% - 36% interest from you, nobody wants to help. Be persistent, and fight for everything you can. These companies count on you giving up.*

Removing Same Name Information

It is common for people with the same name to have their credit data merged. This is caused by a simple data entry error, but it can be living hell for you get it sorted out. Let's say that your name is John Smith and you live in Rhode Island. How many other John Smiths are out there?

Hundreds! If you live in Rhode Island, and see suspicious items on your report from a John Smith in Texas, something is wrong. Credit reporting agencies want to limit their potential liability, and are therefore reluctant to change anything regardless of what proof that you send. Before you go to court, here are a couple of things that might work. We have advised some folks to present a **same name affidavit** to the credit reporting agencies. This document simply confirms that you have provided proof of your identity to a notary, who is an officer of the state.

You present this affidavit under the penalty of perjury. *If the credit reporting agency fails to recognize the laws of notary, they are setting themselves up for a potential contempt of court action.* After all, the notary is empowered by the state to define and notarize the proof of identity. If two people have the exact same name, and they both have a certain debt reported on their credit reports, this is the only way to get the credit bureaus to know who you are.

Sometimes handwriting comparisons have to take place to prove who someone is. But a same name affidavit is the same as if a Judge told everyone on the face of the earth that you are Tom Jones. This is challenging the creditors to prove who purchased a particular item. I once had a client named Juan Gomez. He was denied for a loan because the mortgage company said he had a judgment in Miami, Florida on his credit record.

All materials contained here-in are the property of the R.Sauger Company under US Copyright TX0005895316/203-12-16 or otherwise referred to as being available under the US Freedom of Information Act.

(Our, Juan Gomez had never even been to Miami.) He tried everything to get them to remove the judgment from his credit report, but with no luck. Finally I had him fill out a same name affidavit. We then asked the clerk of court to pull up the case where someone named Juan Gomez had a judgment rendered. We also asked the clerk for the social security number of the Juan Gomez who was in the court in Miami – and it did not match my client's social security.

We provided the social security number associated with the judgment, along with the same name affidavit, to the underwriter at the mortgage company. We proved that the judgment was not my client's, and now everyone down the line knew that our Juan Gomez was not the Juan Gomez who had a judgment in Miami. I even had to have a "serious" discussion with the Sr- Underwriter who at first refused to accept anything. The threat of being charged with "contempt of court" soon convinced him that he didn't want to go into that room. Amazing how people react to knowledge!

Proving the Debt

Man, oh man, this is really interesting. In the beginning of this book, I talked about the Fair Credit Reporting Act (FCRA) and the Fair Debt Collection Practices Act (FDCPA), and now everything comes full circle. So far I have talked about small claims courts, lawsuits, medical bills, debt collections and even our nosy neighbors. But this may be the single most important segment of the whole book.

Under the FDCPA, you have the right to ask a collector or creditor to prove that the amount owed is accurate. In the process of having the debt proven, you are entitled to see an accounting history of the debt. Upon request, the creditor is required to provide *a complete record of all of your payments and purchases.*

Think about this for a minute – they must be able to show when you opened the account, every purchase you made from the account, and every time you made a payment to the account. But I have found that almost no collector can do that. Why? Because, they don't have the information.

Your records are probably long gone, and this can give you a very important advantage. The *only* way that you can force the credit reporting agencies to delete errors on your report is by following this process.

1.) You ask the Credit Reporting Agency to **verify** the information being reported as accurate, which they do about 95% of the time. What you get back is an updated credit report with comments *"we have checked this with the creditor and this account is being reported properly".*

2.) Once you get a verification of the information as being accurate, then you send a registered letter to the creditor (furnisher of information) asking them to **validate** the debt. In most cases they are unable to furnish this information.

All materials contained here-in are the property of the R.Sauger Company under US Copyright TX0005895316/203-12-16 or otherwise referred to as being available under the US Freedom of Information Act.

3.) If you have not heard from the creditor for 30 days, gather the copy of your validation letter and the green receipts from the post office, and send copies of them to the credit reporting agency. In a cover letter ask them how they can verify a debt as accurate, when the creditor has not been able to prove the debt.

4.) This usually takes care of deletions. However, if this doesn't work you can take the credit reporting agency to court. When you request a full accounting history, the creditor or collector will sometimes send you copies of a few of your statements. Often they select the most recent statements that only show over limit and late fees. Because they usually do not have a clue that this is what you are looking for, these statements *might* help you determine the date on which you were first late (date of first delinquency).

5.) *If they cannot show the date of first delinquency,* you can ask them to delete the negative entry from your credit report *because no one can prove when it was first late*. If they can't prove the debt, they are required by law to remove it from your credit file. The date of opening and/or the date of first delinquency provided by the collection agency are often shown as the date that on which the collector received the account. Is that accurate? *Not at all.*

This is called aging an account, which is a Federal violation. See Chapter 7 for more on Aging Accounts. *If you do determine the date of first delinquency,* you just might find out that the debt is *time-barred,* or past the when the debt can be legally collected. **BUT**, that is only a defense and you really have to be on top of the situation to learn.

Aging an Account

Okay, okay, I know you have heard this over and over again – but if you learn only one thing from this entire book, it should be this: *on what date was your account first late and never caught up?* The date of initial delinquency is the most common error on credit reports today. Why? Well because a collection agency probably *does not have this information*, they cannot properly report it. In my workshops and seminars, I tell my students that the single most important question they ask themselves is *"What was the first date I stopped paying on this account?"*

Why is this so important? Under Federal Law, you can have derogatory entries on your credit file for *only seven years*. That's correct. Your sentence to "credit prison" has a maximum of seven years, and the clock starts on the date you first became delinquent. After seven years, your credit returns back to normal (providing you are paying bills on time.) Bankruptcy and other legal records can remain for ten years.

If a credit bureau reports a date that is later than the first delinquency, that is called *aging the account*. Now, keep in mind that these aging violations are on almost everyone's credit report. They show up like ants at a picnic when little Jimmy spills the maple syrup. Aging your account is a violation of your federal rights, and it carries a mandated fine of $1,000 payable to you, if you are the victim.

All materials contained here-in are the property of the R.Sauger Company under US Copyright TX0005895316/203-12-16 or otherwise referred to as being available under the US Freedom of Information Act.

A bill collector is subject to the requirements of the Fair Debt Collection Practices Act and can also be in violation of the Fair Credit Reporting Act.

Quick! When does your seven-year reporting period begin? If you don't know the answer to this yet, you may want to start this book over from the beginning.

Time-Barred Accounts

It is quite possible for an account to be time-barred, or beyond the statute of limitations for collections in your state, but still be reported on your credit report. This is the single most violation of Federal Law on the majority of credit reports. But what do we do about this, Charley? Well, the Truth in Lending Act (TILA) says that if a debt has become time-barred and is still being reported on your credit report, this could be construed as a "deceptive means of collection".

A clever dispute letter or smart attorney can easily get the debt removed from your credit report. How common is the practice of collecting on time-barred accounts? Here is an excerpt of a press release describing how a major debt collection firm "reported accounts using later-than-actual delinquency dates," incurring a $1.5 million civilian penalty.

For Release: May 13, 2004

NCO Group to Pay Largest FCRA Civil Penalty to Date

One of the nation's largest debt-collection firms will pay $1.5 million to settle Federal Trade Commission charges that it violated the Fair Credit Reporting Act (FCRA) by reporting inaccurate information about consumer accounts to credit bureaus. The civil penalty against Pennsylvania-based NCO Group, Inc. is the largest civil penalty ever obtained in a FCRA case.

According to the FTC's complaint, defendants NCO Group, Inc.; NCO Financial Systems, Inc.; and NCO Portfolio Management, Inc. violated Section 623(a)(5) of the FCRA, which specifies that any entity that reports information to credit bureaus about a delinquent consumer account that has been placed for collection or written off must report the actual month and year the account first became delinquent. In turn, this date is used by the credit bureaus to measure the maximum seven-year reporting period the FCRA mandates.

The provision helps ensure that outdated debts – debts that are beyond this seven-year reporting period – do not appear on a consumer's credit report. Violations of this provision of the FCRA are subject to civil penalties of $2,500 per violation.

All materials contained here-in are the property of the R.Sauger Company under US Copyright TX0005895316/203-12-16 or otherwise referred to as being available under the US Freedom of Information Act.

The FTC charges that NCO reported accounts using later-than-actual delinquency dates. Reporting later-than-actual dates may cause negative information to remain in a consumer's credit file beyond the seven-year reporting period permitted by the FCRA for most information. When this occurs, consumers' credit scores may be lowered, possibly resulting in their rejection for credit or their having to pay a higher interest rate.

The proposed consent decree orders the defendants to pay civil penalties of $1.5 million and permanently bars them from reporting later-than-actual delinquency dates to credit bureaus in the future. Additionally, NCO is required to implement a program to monitor all complaints received to ensure that reporting errors are corrected quickly. The consent agreement also contains standard recordkeeping and other requirements to assist the FTC in monitoring the defendants compliance.(FTC File No. 992-3012) (Civil Action No. 04-2041)

I ask the burning question again: when is your account past the statute of limitations (SOL)? Got a clue? To answer this question, you must determine **the date your account was first late and never got caught up**, and then add the number of years of your state's SOL. If your debt is past the SOL, then your account is time-barred, and can no longer be legally collected. This is important stuff, and I will keep banging it into your head throughout this book. I have included at the end of this book the Statute of Limitations for every State. USE IT.

You might be thinking, "This old goat has nothing else to say! He just keeps telling me I need to find out when my account was first late." Well, I really want to make sure you understand that the SOL refers to the time in which a debt can be legally collected. Let's say you just got a collection letter, for a credit card to which you have not made a payment for five years. They tell you that they will accept half of the amount owed, but you do not pay them. Now the collector decides that because you chose to ignore their friendly offer, they will file a lawsuit against you.

But you just told me that because the debt is beyond the SOL, I don't legally have to pay it! That is correct – **you don't legally have to pay, but that doesn't stop them from trying to collect**. Let's say the collector files a lawsuit, and because you didn't understand how the system works, you ignored the lawsuit. **If you do not show up in court, he wins by default.** Now you have a judgment against you for a debt that you legally did not have to pay.

I know it's tough, but please think about this again, because it's so important! The only defense you have against a lawsuit for a time-barred debt is the fact that it is time-barred. You simply show up in court, and state that this debt is time-barred per the statutes of your state. But **do not fail to show up in court**, otherwise they get a default judgment on a debt you might not legally owe.

Re-Aging Your Account

This is a technique you can use to clean up your credit history and improve your credit score, particularly **if you had a brief problem and you're back in control**.

All materials contained here-in are the property of the R.Sauger Company under US Copyright TX0005895316/203-12-16 or otherwise referred to as being available under the US Freedom of Information Act.

Basically, when an account is re-aged, it is no longer considered past due. A big "late" blemish comes off your account when the creditor simply re-labels the account "current." Let's say you are three months late on one of your credit cards. If you can convince the credit card provider to re-age your account, it's as if those three months never happened. You still owe the same amount of money, but the late fees stop and you are no longer considered delinquent. Your missed payments are simply ignored.

Getting a creditor to re-age your account is not easy—and it's not something you can do often. The best approach is to offer some form of payment immediately, plus offer a schedule of more-than-minimum payments, in exchange for the re-aging. The government has set out guidelines for re-aging through the Federal Financial Institutions Examination Council (FFIEC). The FFIEC is an inter-agency government body that prescribes uniform principles, standards and report forms for the federal examination of financial institutions and makes recommendations to promote uniformity in the supervision of financial institutions.

According to the FFIEC, for an open-ended loan (like a credit card account) to be eligible for re-aging, it must meet the following conditions:

1.) The account should exist for at least nine months;

2.) The borrower should show a willingness and ability to repay the loan;

3.) The borrower should make at least three consecutive monthly payments or an equivalent lump sum payment;

4.) A loan should not be re-aged more than once within any 12-month period;

5.) New credit should not be extended to the borrower until the balance falls below the pre-delinquency credit limit.

A word of caution: there is no point in begging a creditor to re-age your account if there is *any* chance that you will wind up delinquent again in the near future. Save your energy and time for other credit-saving efforts! However, if for the foreseeable future you are committed to making at least the minimum monthly payments, *on time*, then your first step is to contact your creditor in writing. Tell the company;

1) Why you were late on the payments in question; and

2) Why you know you'll be able to pay on time in the future.

Be sure to get any agreement to re-age your account *in writing*. Many consumers have been told over the phone that a creditor will re-age their account, only to discover that the re-aging never takes place. If the card company agrees to re-age your account but won't put the agreement in writing, you can take matters into your own hands. Ask the customer service agent to give you the name and mailing address of his or her supervisor.

All materials contained here-in are the property of the R.Sauger Company under US Copyright TX0005895316/203-12-16 or otherwise referred to as being available under the US Freedom of Information Act.

Then write a letter that describes your conversation in detail, and state that you believe this conversation was an agreement to re-age your account. Send the letter via certified mail, with a return receipt, to the supervisor.

Rehabilitating Student Loans

You should be aware that statute of limitations (SOL) laws do not apply to government student loans (GSLs), and GSLs are not dischargeable under bankruptcy unless the debt is seven years old or the debtor experiences an undue hardship in repaying the loan. A GSL is one debt that will never go away until it is paid or settled.

However, if you get behind on a student loan from the government, you can rehabilitate that loan by making **nine payments on time**. According to the Higher Education Act, after receiving those nine payments, the US Government will direct Sallie Mae to delete the entire prior payment history from your credit record.

Getting A Credit Reporting Agency To Correct Your Report

This is where all of your studying begins to show results. Ask yourself this question, "If the credit reporting agency only reports what is furnished to them, then how can I get them to correct my report?" Remember that credit reporting agencies (CRAs) are for-profit companies that are paid by creditors. They will always favor the creditor over you, and **in some cases CRAs may refuse to delete or correct your credit report.**

So you have found the errors in your credit report, and now you want to ask the CRA to fix them. This four-step process is the only one I have found that works. Remember this: The little girl that works in Atlanta or at the other Credit Reporting Agencies has a stack of letters put on her desk every morning. Sometimes, you get lucky and this girl really reads your letters and deletes some entries.

But, sometimes you get the "village idiot" that thinks she has the power of "The Gods" and just won't delete anything. However, is you are persistent, you just might find the right little girl that will delete. So, in your process follow these directions.

STEP 1 – VERIFY

First, write a very nice letter to the credit reporting agency and ask them to verify the information that is reported to them as accurate. **Do not tell them what you think is wrong**, because they will simply have it corrected and you gain nothing. The CRA will usually send a generic response in reply to your first letter. In the summer of 2008, an executive told the Senate Banking Commission under oath that TransUnion had "off-shored" their dispute processing to the Philippines, India and Trinidad to lower their costs.

All materials contained here-in are the property of the R.Sauger Company under US Copyright TX0005895316/203-12-16 or otherwise referred to as being available under the US Freedom of Information Act.

This means that if you sent a letter to TransUnion, they did not forward it to Trinidad; they only forwarded notification of your request, with a code number. The worker in Trinidad was simply instructed to respond to your initial request with a pre-written form letter – they have a version for medical disputes, one for repossessions, one for collections, etc.

STEP 2 – VALIDATE

Within two weeks of sending the first letter to the credit reporting agencies, send another letter via **Certified Mail** with a **Return Receipt Request** to the furnisher of information (creditor) asking them to **validate** the account (have it proven as you have learned). In most cases, they will be unable to validate the information because the records are long gone. Make sure you keep the green return receipt card that proves that the creditor received the letter.

STEP 3 – REQUEST REMOVAL

If you do not receive a response within 30 days from the date on your return receipt), then the furnisher of information has **failed to validate your debt**. Your next task is to send a letter to the credit reporting agency asking them how the furnisher of information can verify the past-due information as accurate when they have not proven the debt (by validating it.) With the letter, include a copy of the letter that you sent to the furnisher of information, along with a copy of the signed green receipt card that proves that the furnisher of information got your letter. *In most cases, the credit bureaus will now delete the entry.*

STEP 4 – IF THEY DON'T RESPOND

Sometimes the CRA just won't comply. Knowing that there are no "credit cops", the furnisher of information may want to play games and do absolutely nothing. What you do next depends entirely on you. **Ask yourself how much it is worth to you to save a couple hundreds of dollars each month by getting a higher credit score.** You can accept the system and continue give away money – or you can fight back. I don't think it's a tough choice, but it is a decision that only you can make.

If the CRA does not fix your credit report after failing to validate, your next step may be to play "footsie" and repeat Step 2, sending another demand for proof of the debt. Or you may decide to stop the charades immediately. If you want to play hardball, go right to step five.

All materials contained here-in are the property of the R.Sauger Company under US Copyright TX0005895316/203-12-16 or otherwise referred to as being available under the US Freedom of Information Act.

STEP 5 – PLAY HARDBALL

Here is where you can lower the boom and make people jump! Your first action is to go to your local small claims court and pick up a couple blank small claims forms. Now, on the front of each form is a section for "statement of claim", which is where you write your complaint. In this section you state that you are suing the furnisher of information (creditor) for violation of a specific federal law.

Here is where you really shine! *Instead of filing the lawsuit with the court, simply have your signature on the first page of the small claims form notarized.* This is why Step 5 is clever: when you have your signature notarized, you are simply swearing under penalty of perjury that you are you. *The notary only witnesses your signature*; they do not notarize the wording of the document. They are not attorneys, nor do they represent the court. Now you send the notarized copy of the first page of your small claims form to the bill collector or furnisher of information that is refusing to update your information.

You have simply put them on notice that you are *serious*. How does it work? Well, imagine what would be like to be the office manager who receives you document by certified mail: *"Hmmmmmm...this is a lawsuit! I'd better look into this file right away because he is serious. If a court finds that we're in violation of federal law, we'll get fined $1,000, and it can't be appealed. Do we want to pay an attorney to represent us when we can – and probably will – lose? Best thing to do is just delete this line from this guy's credit files, and avoid expensive litigation."*

This method has done wonders for many of my clients. I talked to one of our local attorneys and they thought this was a brilliant way to get someone's attention. That is the "crux" of this entire scenario: no one pays attention until you hit them over the head. I rest my case. Now you can see how and why average folks get so disheartened when they try to raise their credit scores or improve their credit. *You must remember that it is you against the system – and you can win.*

Repairing your own credit requires a tremendous amount of knowledge and perseverance, and you are to be commended for getting this far. Now, because you've paying attention, I won't ask you again, *"When was your account first late?"* Surely you already know that date by now, so I am going to let you off of the hook.

Injunctive Relief

That means, the judge has the ability to order the CRA to delete the information pending the outcome of some lawsuit, etc. So I asked around about how this could work in a situation. You could file for injunctive relief without there ever even being a lawsuit. Just prepare a motion seeking temporary injunctive relief and file it with the Clerk of the Court.

All materials contained here-in are the property of the R.Sauger Company under US Copyright TX0005895316/203-12-16 or otherwise referred to as being available under the US Freedom of Information Act.

Here is some sample language.

COUNT I – PERMANENT INJUNCTION

49) Plaintiffs re-allege the allegations set forth in Paragraphs 1 through 10 hereinabove.
50) The information contained in the Plaintiff's credit files is incorrect.
51) Without permanent removal of such inaccurate information, there is no remedy at law for Plaintiff
52) Plaintiff's damages are irreparable unless all inaccurate information is permanently changed.
53) Injunctive relief is provided by 15 U.S.C §1681.

THEREFORE Plaintiffs request that the Court, mandates to enjoin Defendants to render Plaintiffs credit report to be accurate.

In the first few paragraphs, just lay out the basics for your claim and ask for the judge to issue an injunction to make it accurate. The best part about this strategy is that since the CRA is not being sued for any money, they likely won't even show up to fight your injunction.

After the judge signs your injunction order, you mail a copy by certified mail to the CRA legal department and demand immediate deletion per the order of the court. If they want to fight you, they would actually have to go through the trouble of getting a lawyer in your location and digging up all the info as to why it should be on there.

It will never happen. They will just delete it and not do a thing. The beauty of this strategy is that you get the deletions, the CRA does not feel the need to fight since the court is not ruling that they need to pay money. An injunction hearing is typically something quick that you can get without filing a full blown lawsuit.

17. GETTING STARTED..

Mental Preparation

If you are like most people, you just don't know where to start – that is why you prefer to ignore your debts, even as they get bigger and bigger. Maybe you are waiting for your "smart" brother-in-law to come over and tell you what to do. After all, isn't he the top used car salesman at the local "Honest Al's' used car lot? OK, take a deep breath. You only have to do this one step at a time.

All materials contained here-in are the property of the R.Sauger Company under US Copyright TX0005895316/203-12-16 or otherwise referred to as being available under the US Freedom of Information Act.

Credit restoration does not happen overnight. Depending on how many items on your report are in need of attention, you may work at it from 60 days to 2 years. It is helpful to look at it *as the first step in an overall plan for building, or rebuilding your financial future.* Increasing your access to consumer credit is not about buying more things for your house! When used properly, good credit is the most powerful tool of leverage for creating personal wealth you can possibly have at your disposal.

To accelerate the process of rebuilding good credit, you must eliminate all of the hindrances that you can, regardless of the source.

See the big picture. If you have a big job ahead of you, look at it as part of a larger financial planning program. Staying focused on your long-term objective will help keep you from becoming discouraged should you lose a battle here or there. There are many battles in any war; you don't have to win them *all* to emerge as the winner. And just as in a real war, there is always more than one way to attack. Before you begin, *make a commitment to yourself to follow through on every step.*

Make Three Piles

As your first exercise in Debt Management, I want you to take out that box of collection letters you have accumulated and begin to get it in order. The information in this book will help you to start separating these collection letters into three piles:

(1) These debts are mine but I don't have any money to pay. **(2)**

These debts are mine but I don't owe this much money. **(3)** These

debts are not mine.

Be honest with yourself, and have the courage to take control of this pile of letters. In no time, you will have reduced this pile of "misery" to something that you can deal with.

Organization And Planning

Organization is crucial to any big campaign. It's easy to get discouraged when you realize that you may have to contact each major bureau for each item in question; that you will have to follow up on each and every request; and that you may have to write letters to the original creditor at the same time. It's easy to get confused about what you said to whom, which letter was sent where on what date.

There are many ways to organize your efforts, but here is a simple system you can use to stay on top of things without spending more than a few dollars.

All materials contained here-in are the property of the R.Sauger Company under US Copyright TX0005895316/203-12-16 or otherwise referred to as being available under the US Freedom of Information Act.

You will need:

(1) Three hanging file holders (one for each of the three major CRAs)

(2) Standard file folders

(3) Calendar (some prefer their electronic or notebook day timer)

(4) Notepad to keep a log of important events and conversations

First, grab a file folder. On the tab, write the item you are going to be working on and place the folder in the hanging holder for the appropriate bureau. Each item that you are going to work on should have its own file folder. For example, if you have three accounts that you will be dealing with in your Equifax report, you will have three file folders in the Equifax holder.

Every time you send or receive a correspondence about that item, a copy of it will need to be placed in that folder. Next you will need to tear some blank sheets of paper out of your notepad and tape one to the front of each folder. This will be your log to record the date of every letter mailed and received, as well as the date and content of phone conversations related to the item in the folder.

Create a separate journal on the notepad. At some point, you may begin dealing directly with the original creditor or a collection agent. Every time you have a telephone conversation, you must document the conversation by recording the name and title of the person with whom you spoke, key points discussed and what you agreed to do. You should also record the name of the person's supervisor, and that direct phone number if possible. This kind of documentation is very important, especially if you ever have to go to small claims court and make a case.

Always assume they will be documenting their end, so you need to as well. Follow all of this advice and you will be prepared with documentation to the hilt.

Don't Show Your Hand –

Never mention in word or in writing that you are attempting to repair your credit. If you telephone the CRA to order your credit reports or to confirm their mailing address, you will most likely reach their automated phone system. However, if you do speak to a representative about any issue, be careful to say nothing that would indicate you are attempting to repair your credit.

The reason for this is to lesson the chance that the bureau will respond to any of your disputes by claiming them to be "frivolous or irrelevant." By law, the only way they can get out of doing reinvestigations is to claim this charge. You don't want to make it easy for them to make this claim.

All materials contained here-in are the property of the R.Sauger Company under US Copyright TX0005895316/203-12-16 or otherwise referred to as being available under the US Freedom of Information Act.

Don't Be Sloppy –

Use a typewriter or word processor to draft your letters. Create your own personal letterhead if you don't have one. Project the image of someone who conducts his or her affairs in a professional manner. It also a very good idea to have someone proofread your letters before sending them.

You want to give the appearance that you taking action on your own initiative, so don't use form letters without changing them. Personalize your letter! Use sample letters as a template from which to draft your own.

Don't Abuse The System –

Just because the law allows you to ask for a re-investigation of questionable items on your report doesn't mean you should write something like, *"It's all wrong! And I'm mad as hell!!!"* on your report and send it back to them charred around the edges. And be careful about disputing multiple issues simultaneously. Unprofessional tactics like these will likely get your file flagged as an attempt at credit repair, or could even result in a fraud alert.

Don't Lie –

No, this is not a sermon – I'm just giving you good advice to follow. Technically, lying on a credit application is a federal crime. In some states, it could also be a crime for you to lie when disputing items in your credit file. I therefore warn you to never lie or make misleading statements when disputing your credit report. Why would you? It is unnecessary to lie when disputing your credit report. Remember, you have the right to dispute your credit report as long as you have reasons to believe that it is not 100% accurate, or is misleading or obsolete.

Don't Be Cheap –

Send every letter by **Certified Mail**, with **Return Receipt Requested**. This means you must go to a post office to mail every letter. Certified mail, with return receipt requested, will cost more than a dollar extra, but it also shows that you are serious about your letter. After the letter is delivered, your postal carrier will bring you a signed card from the recipient with the date they received it. This is the *only* way to have proof that your letter was sent and received. Your post office will provide you with the necessary forms.

Don't Be Vague In Your Disputes –

Be as clear as you can about what you are disputing and the corrective action you want someone to take. Always provide as much supporting documentation as you can. But at the same time, try to sound like "Joe Average" in your letter, not "Joe Expert." Don't go quoting sections of the law and such. Present yourself as a concerned consumer acting on the advice of a friend or family member.

All materials contained here-in are the property of the R.Sauger Company under US Copyright TX0005895316/203-12-16 or otherwise referred to as being available under the US Freedom of Information Act.

Over time, if they are doing nothing, you can escalate the tone of your letters. The most serious approach you can take is to get an attorney to quote the law on your behalf. By this point you are portraying yourself as a concerned citizen who is at the point of taking legal action, and you will have their undivided attention. If you ever go to court, you will have better results if you present yourself as someone who set out to correct a mistake, rather than someone who launching a personal credit fix campaign.

Don't Jump Ahead –

Credit restoration can take time. Systems this big and cumbersome tend to have multiple layers of bureaucratic sediment deposited on them. It can take hours of work to even get the wheels in motion, and you will probably have to wait for weeks for each new revolution to be completed. Follow the steps I have outlined for you, and you will see success. Cleaning up your credit report may seem like a monumental task. But it's not as complicated as you think, and the success rate is high for those who follow this system and take advantage of mistakes made by creditors and credit bureaus. Exercise patience. Look for opportunities. They will first appear as very small cracks.

The Dispute Process

The first weapon in a consumer's war chest is the right to request that a credit reporting agency *reinvestigate* any item contained in his or her credit file. Often referred to as a *dispute*, this right to re-investigate is provided for in The Fair Credit Reporting Act (FCRA). Of all the remedies spelled out by law, a dispute is the easiest to use and the most powerful weapon for removing inaccurate, incomplete and unverifiable information from your credit report.

These re-investigations are requested so often that the CRAs now include a standardized dispute form with each credit report. Section 611 (a)(1)(A) of the FCRA requires that: *"if the completeness or accuracy of any item of information contained in a consumer's file at a consumer reporting agency is disputed by the consumer and the consumer notifies the agency directly of such dispute, the agency shall re-investigate free of charge".*

The CRA must record the current status of the disputed information, or delete the item from the file before within 30 days of receiving notice of the dispute from the consumer. If the item is found to belong to someone else or can no longer be verified, then the agency must immediately delete the item from the consumer's record. The agency does have one chance of escape – but only if you give it to them.

They are not required to reinvestigate an item for which it deems the dispute *frivolous or irrelevant*. Section 611 (a)(3)(A) says: *"...a consumer reporting agency may terminate a re-investigation of information disputed by a consumer under that paragraph if the agency reasonably determines that the dispute by the consumer is frivolous or irrelevant, including by reason of a failure by a consumer to provide sufficient information to investigate the disputed information."*

All materials contained here-in are the property of the R.Sauger Company under US Copyright TX0005895316/203-12-16 or otherwise referred to as being available under the US Freedom of Information Act.

The law requires that an agency notify you within 5 business days if they determine your dispute to be frivolous or irrelevant. The law does not dare to define what the grounds are for making such a determination except for *"failure by a consumer to provide sufficient information to investigate the disputed information."* Yes, that's pretty vague. To insure you don't get tagged as one making frivolous charges, you need to find evidence to support everything you do. But it's usually not hard – any item on your report that is not 100% accurate is disputable, and incorrect items are easily deleted.

The bottom line is that you realize early on that disputes are a "smart weapon" to be used to attack a specific problem. Do not use disputes in a shotgun fashion over your entire credit report – if you do, you are more likely to make people mad and not solve anything. In many cases, even *correctly* reported negative items can be removed through dispute. Often an item will be deleted when the creditor no longer has the original file, or does not have enough staff to investigate whether a dispute is valid or not.

In the past, deleted items sometimes would magically reappear on a consumer's credit file, usually the result of an automatic update to the payment history on an account that still had payment activity. However, Section 611 (a)(5)(C) of the new FCRA does not allow a deleted item to be added again unless the creditor certifies that the information is correct.

18. CONCLUSION..

Beware of "Information Updated" Responses

If you have sent in a number of items, the bureaus may send you back reports that just say "Information updated" or "Creditor has updated." If you get this response, ***don't quit there***. Now is the time to start picking on certain items within the report or related to that account that you know could possibly be due to human error or an account being transferred or sold.

My daughter was the victim of one of these situations. While she was in college she opened a Montgomery Wards account. The account was sold/transferred to a collection agency. Later on, that agency sold it to another agency. Meanwhile, my daughter had been receiving collection notices for almost ten years.

Her first letter to the bureau indicated that she felt the information on her credit report was erroneous because of the account being more than seven years old from the last date of activity. Her initial dispute letter was answered with a typical "information has been updated". She would not settle for that answer and under Section 611(a)(5)(C), her dispute was re-entered. The law is specific. Even though your account can be sold, the statute of limitations (SOL) is specific. "A collection account must be deleted after seven years from the commencement of the initial delinquency."

All materials contained here-in are the property of the R.Sauger Company under US Copyright TX0005895316/203-12-16 or otherwise referred to as being available under the US Freedom of Information Act.

While the credit industry has grown be to a billion dollar industry, there are still only three for-profit companies that manage credit transactions for almost 290 million people. The human error in data entry is mind-boggling – so you owe it to yourself and your family to learn about this industry and how it can affect your daily life.

I have seen and witnessed a lot of suffering and unnecessary hardship that resulted from a lack of knowledge about credit. The average American consumer seems to think that his or her credit is no big deal. But the figures do not lie – more and more Americans experience some type of credit problem every year.

I think we have a lot to learn from immigrants who arrive in the US without a job, without experience and having a hard time with English. I have seen many cases where after just five years, they hold multiple jobs, own the home they are living in, and have a decent car in the driveway. These individuals took the time to understand that our system rewards people for paying their bills on time. My wife is foreign-born, and I am constantly surprised by how the world appears through her eyes.

I have a lot to learn. The lesson is simple: if you have a record of paying your bills on time, the system will tell the world, and you can usually buy a home, car or land with little or no money down. So if the system works for people who haven't had the chances that you have, then the system will also work for you and your family.

By reading this book, you now know more than most people ever will about how our credit system works. Many credit industry professionals have gotten angry with me because I'm "spilling the secrets." But I feel strongly that this is information that everyone should know. Hardly anyone goes to the effort of gathering all of the paperwork, or challenging the powers that be. **Remember: you have more power than you think!** You do not have to endure harassment, and you don't have to stay in credit prison forever. You can begin plotting your escape today. Now I'm going to ask you about your credit prison sentence one last time:

When does the commencement of your 7-year term of delinquency begin?

When you have the answer to this question, then you are ready to begin the rest of your credit life.

GOOD LUCK!

Regis P Sauger
Author/Speaker

All materials contained here-in are the property of the R.Sauger Company under US Copyright TX0005895316/203-12-16 or otherwise referred to as being available under the US Freedom of Information Act.

Following are the Statute of Limitations for each State. These are included for your easy reference.

ALABAMA
INTEREST RATE: Legal: 6%, Judgment: 12%
STATUTE OF LIMITATIONS (IN YEARS)
Open Acct.: 3, Written Contract: 6, Domestic Judgment: 20 and Foreign Judgment: 20
BAD CHECK LAWS (CIVIL PENALTY)
Greater of $10 or Actual Bank Charges
GENERAL GARNISHMENT EXEMPTIONS
75% of wages are exempt from garnishment
COLLECTION AGENCY BOND & LICENSE Bond:
No
License: Yes
Fee:
$25 - Population under 20,000
$100 - Population over 20,000
Exemption for out-of-state collectors: Business License not required for out-of-state agency.

ALASKA
INTEREST RATE
Legal: 10.5%, Judgment: 10.5% or contractual
STATUTE OF LIMITATIONS (IN YEARS)
Open Account: 3, Sale of Goods: 4, Written Contract: 6, Domestic Judgment: 10 Foreign Judgment: 10
BAD CHECK LAWS (CIVIL PENALTY) Damages in amount equal to $100 or triple the amount of the check whichever is greater but no more than $1000 over the amount of the check.
GENERAL GARNISHMENT EXEMPTIONS
75% of employee's weekly net income or $402.50 whichever is more.
COLLECTION AGENCY BOND & LICENSE
Bond: $5000 License: Yes
Fee:
$100 - Application
$200 - Agency Biennially

ARIZONA
INTEREST RATE
Legal: 10%
106
Judgment: 10% or contractual

All materials contained here-in are the property of the R.Sauger Company under US Copyright TX0005895316/203-12-16 or otherwise referred to as being available under the US Freedom of Information Act.

STATUTE OF LIMITATIONS (IN YEARS)
Open Acct.: 3, Written Contract: 6 in Az. - 4 outside Az., Domestic Judgment: 5-additional 5 upon request (indefinitely), Foreign Judgment: 4
BAD CHECK LAWS (CIVIL PENALTY)
Twice the amount of check, costs of suit, reasonable attorney fees.
GENERAL GARNISHMENT EXEMPTIONS
See federal law.
COLLECTION AGENCY BOND & LICENSE
Bond: $10,000 minimum (based on gross income)
License: Yes
Fee:
$1500 Application Fee
$600 Annual Fee
$23 per Officers/Managers

ARKANSAS
INTEREST RATE
Legal: 6% or 5 points above the Fed. discount rate
Judgment: Contract rate or 10% per annum whichever is greater
STATUTE OF LIMITATIONS (IN YEARS)
Open Acct.: 3, Written Contract: 5 (partial payment stops the statute from running (This applies to a WRITTEN ACCOUNT ONLY)
Sale of Goods: (UCC-2) – 4, Domestic Judgment: 10 – Renewable, Foreign Judgment: 10
BAD CHECK LAWS (CIVIL PENALTY)
Twice amount of check - prior to double charge - can start out with $15 charge per NSF check after 30 days.
GENERAL GARNISHMENT EXEMPTIONS
$500 head of family; $200 single, includes personal property except clothing.
COLLECTION AGENCY BOND & LICENSE
Bond: $5000 to $25000
License: Yes
Fee: $125 - $5 each employee

CALIFORNIA
INTEREST RATE
Legal: 10%
Judgment: 10% (Unless otherwise contracted)
STATUTE OF LIMITATIONS (IN YEARS)
Open Acct.: Reduced to writing-4, Open Acct.: No writing-2, Written Contract: 4
Domestic Judgment: 10 (renewable at 10), Foreign Judgment: 10 (commencing with judgment debtor's commencement of CA. residence.)
BAD CHECK LAWS (CIVIL PENALTY)
Amount due, Treble damages - minimum $100 maximum $1500 per check
GENERAL GARNISHMENT EXEMPTIONS
See federal law. Exemptions for necessaries of life.
COLLECTION AGENCY BOND & LICENSE

All materials contained here-in are the property of the R.Sauger Company under US Copyright TX0005895316/203-12-16 or otherwise referred to as being available under the US Freedom of Information Act.

No license or bond required.

COLORADO
INTEREST RATE
Legal: 8%
Judgment: 8% (or higher if specified in contract or note)
STATUTE OF LIMITATIONS (IN YEARS)
Open Acct.: 3, Written Contract: 6 (signed promissory note), Written Contract Goods Services: 3
Domestic Judgment
District Court-20 (renewable every 20), County Court-6 (renewable every 6), Foreign Judgment: 6 in CO.
BAD CHECK LAWS (CIVIL PENALTY)
Treble Damages & Reasonable Fees
GENERAL GARNISHMENT EXEMPTIONS
See federal law.
COLLECTION AGENCY BOND & LICENSE
Bond: $12,000 - 20,000
License: Yes
Fee: Determined by collection agency board
Exemption for out-of-state collectors: Out of state collectors are exempt if [1] collecting only by interstate means (phone, fax, mail); [2] have no Colorado client; and [3] are regulated and licensed in the state in which they reside.

CONNECTICUT
INTEREST RATE
Legal: 8%
Judgment: 10%
STATUTE OF LIMITATIONS (IN YEARS)
Open Acct.: 3, Written Contract: 6, Oral Contract: 3,
Domestic Judgment: 20/25, Small Claims Judgment: 10/15, Foreign Judgment: 20
BAD CHECK LAWS (CIVIL PENALTY)
Personal liability of signatory on corporate claims unless signed in corporate capacity.
108
GENERAL GARNISHMENT EXEMPTIONS
25% you may garnish disposable earnings each week, or 40 x fed. min. hourly wage, whichever is less.
COLLECTION AGENCY BOND & LICENSE
Bond: $5000
License: Yes
Fee:
$200 Yearly
$50 Investigation

All materials contained here-in are the property of the R.Sauger Company under US Copyright TX0005895316/203-12-16 or otherwise referred to as being available under the US Freedom of Information Act.

DELAWARE
INTEREST RATE
Legal + Judgment -
Federal Reserve Discount Rate Plus 5% Points
STATUTE OF LIMITATIONS (IN YEARS)
Sale of Goods: 4, Open Acct.: 4, Written Contract: 3
Domestic Judgment: No provision
Foreign Judgment: No provision
BAD CHECK LAWS (CIVIL PENALTY)
Amount due, cost of suit, protest fees
GENERAL GARNISHMENT EXEMPTIONS
85% of disposable earnings or disposable earnings minus $150 weekly according to schedule.
COLLECTION AGENCY BOND & LICENSE
Bond: No
License: Merc. License
Fee: $50 Yearly

DISTRICT OF COLUMBIA
INTEREST RATE
Legal: 6%
Judgment: 70% of interest rates on taxes to IRS
STATUTE OF LIMITATIONS (IN YEARS)
Open Acct.: 3, Written Contract: 3,
Domestic Judgment: 20, Foreign Judgment: Foreign Statute
BAD CHECK LAWS (CIVIL PENALTY)
Amount Due - Protest Fees
GENERAL GARNISHMENT EXEMPTIONS
See federal law. D.C. Government employees are not attachable.
COLLECTION AGENCY BOND & LICENSE
Bond: No
License: No
109
Fee: No

FLORIDA
INTEREST RATE
Judgment: 10% or up to 18% if contractual
STATUTE OF LIMITATIONS (IN YEARS)
Open Acct.: 4, Written Contract: 5,
Domestic Judgment: 7 Renewable, Foreign Judgment: 5 if not recorded in-state
BAD CHECK LAWS (CIVIL PENALTY)
GENERAL GARNISHMENT EXEMPTIONS
See federal law except 100% head of household.
Liberal Homestead Exemption - 1st $1,000 of automobile
COLLECTION AGENCY BOND & LICENSE
Bond: Yes - $50,000 (Commercial)

All materials contained here-in are the property of the R.Sauger Company under US Copyright TX0005895316/203-12-16 or otherwise referred to as being available under the US Freedom of Information Act.

License: Yes
Fee: Yes
$200 - Registration
$50 - Investigation
$200 - Renewal
Exemption for out-of-state collectors:
Registration is required for out-of-state collectors if
[1] soliciting accounts;
[2] if client (creditor, its affiliate or subsidiary) has an office in Florida.

GEORGIA
INTEREST RATE
Legal: 7%
Judgment: 12%
Commercial Accounts: 18%
STATUTE OF LIMITATIONS (IN YEARS)
Open Acct.: 4, Written Contract: 6
Domestic Judgment: 7, Foreign Judgment: 5
BAD CHECK LAWS (CIVIL PENALTY)
After 10 day written demand double damages up to $500 and service charge of
$20 or 5%, whichever is greater,
GENERAL GARNISHMENT EXEMPTIONS
See federal law. City, County & State employees may be garnished.
COLLECTION AGENCY BOND & LICENSE
Bond: No
110
License: No
Fee: No

HAWAII
INTEREST RATE
Legal: 10% (no written contract)
Judgment: 10% (no written contract)
STATUTE OF LIMITATIONS (IN YEARS)
Sale of Goods: 6, Open Acct.: 6, Written Contract: 6
Domestic Judgment: 10, Foreign Judgment: 6 for regis./10 after Registration
BAD CHECK LAWS (CIVIL PENALTY)
Damages equal to $100 or triple amount of check, not to exceed $500.
GENERAL GARNISHMENT EXEMPTIONS 95% of 1st $100, 90% of 2nd $100,
80% net wages in excess of $200 per mo. or federal limits whichever is greater
COLLECTION AGENCY BOND & LICENSE
Bond: $25,000/$15,000 each branch
License: Registration with 'DCCA' required for consumer, not commercial, collections
Fee:
$ 25 - Application
$ 80 - Registration
$ 50 - Compliance

All materials contained here-in are the property of the R.Sauger Company under US Copyright TX0005895316/203-12-16 or otherwise referred to as being available under the US Freedom of Information Act.

$155 for 2 years

IDAHO
INTEREST RATE
Legal: 12%
Judgment: 10.875% plus the base rate
STATUTE OF LIMITATIONS (IN YEARS)
Open Acct.: 4, Oral Contract: 4, Written Contract: 5
Domestic Judgment: 5 renewable, Foreign Judgment: 6 renewable
BAD CHECK LAWS (CIVIL PENALTY)
Triple amount of check up to $500 over the check amount
GENERAL GARNISHMENT EXEMPTIONS
See federal law.
COLLECTION AGENCY BOND & LICENSE
Bond: $5,000 initial
License: Yes
Fee: $100 -permit fee $50 - renewal
Exemption for out-of-state collectors: Out-of-state collectors may qualify for a special license if [1] only collecting for client; and [2] are licensed and bonded by any state

---

ILLINOIS
INTEREST RATE
Legal: 5%
Judgment: 9%
STATUTE OF LIMITATIONS (IN YEARS)
Sales (UCC): 4, Open Acct.: 5, Written Contract: 10,
Domestic Judgment: 20, Foreign Judgment: Same as foreign jurisdiction
BAD CHECK LAWS (CIVIL PENALTY) Triple check amount up to $500, attorney fees & court costs.
GENERAL GARNISHMENT EXEMPTIONS
15% of gross wages or disposable earnings for workweek up to 45 x fed. min. hourly wage, whichever is greater.
COLLECTION AGENCY BOND & LICENSE
Bond: $25,000
License: Yes
Fee:
$750 - Original
$750 - Renewal
Exemption for out-of-state collectors:
Out-of-state collectors MAY be exempt if
[1] not soliciting accounts in Illinois;
[2] their state of residence has laws which provide similar reciprocity (allow outof-state agencies to collect only); and
[3] the state in which the non-Illinois agency resides extends the same privileges to out-of-state agencies.

All materials contained here-in are the property of the R.Sauger Company under US Copyright TX0005895316/203-12-16 or otherwise referred to as being available under the US Freedom of Information Act.

INDIANA
INTEREST RATE
Legal: 8%
Judgment: 8%
STATUTE OF LIMITATIONS (IN YEARS)
Open Acct.: 6 ,Written Contract for payment of money: 6, Written Contract (other than payment of money): 10, Written Contract for sale of goods: 4
Domestic Judgment:
10 on real estate, 20 against the person, Foreign Judgment: 10
BAD CHECK LAWS (CIVIL PENALTY)
Triple check amount up to $500 over check amount, + attorney fees & interest up to 18% per annum or triple check amount + attorney fees and interest at 8% per annum.
GENERAL WAGE GARNISHMENT EXEMPTIONS 75% of disposable earnings for work week or the amount of 30 x fed. min. hourly wage, whichever is greater.
112
COLLECTION AGENCY BOND & LICENSE
Bond: $5000 each office
License: Yes
Fee:
$100 plus $5 per annum, each unlicenced employee
$30 branch office
$80 - Renewal
Exemption for out-of-state collectors:
Out-of-state collectors are exempt from licensing if
[1] collecting for a non-resident creditor; and
[2] collection activities limited to interstate communications (phone, fax, mail).

....

IOWA
INTEREST RATE
Legal: 5%
Judgment: 10%
STATUTE OF LIMITATIONS (IN YEARS)
Open Acct.: 5, Written Contract: 10,
Domestic Judgment: 10-can be renewed in the 9th year, Foreign Judgment: 10- can be renewed in the 9th year
BAD CHECK LAWS (CIVIL PENALTY)
Triple check up to $500 over check amount
GENERAL GARNISHMENT EXEMPTIONS
See federal law.
COLLECTION AGENCY BOND & LICENSE
Bond: No
License: No

....

KANSAS
INTEREST RATE
Legal: 10%

All materials contained here-in are the property of the R.Sauger Company under US Copyright TX0005895316/203-12-16 or otherwise referred to as being available under the US Freedom of Information Act.

Judgment: 12%
STATUTE OF LIMITATIONS (IN YEARS)
Open Acct.: 3, Written Contract: 6, Action On Forfeiture: 5
Domestic Judgment: 5 renewable, Foreign Judgment: 5 renewable
BAD CHECK LAWS (CIVIL PENALTY)
Three times check amount not exceeding the check amount by $500 or $100
whichever is greater plus attorney fees
GENERAL GARNISHMENT EXEMPTIONS See Federal Law
Plus other personal property, benefit exemptions, and homestead
COLLECTION AGENCY BOND & LICENSE
Bond: No
License: No

....

KENTUCKY
INTEREST RATE
Legal: 8%
Judgment: 12%
STATUTE OF LIMITATIONS (IN YEARS)
Open Acct.: 5, Written Contract: 15, Oral Contract: 5
Domestic Judgment: 15, Foreign Judgment: 15
BAD CHECK LAWS (CIVIL PENALTY)
N/A
GENERAL GARNISHMENT EXEMPTIONS
75% of disposable income or 30 times the federal minimum hourly wage
(whichever is greater)
COLLECTION AGENCY BOND & LICENSE
Bond: No
License: No
Fee: No

....

LOUISIANA
INTEREST RATE
Legal: 9.75%
Judgment: 9.75%
STATUTE OF LIMITATIONS (IN YEARS)
Open Acct.: 3, Written Contract: 10, Promissory Notes: 5
Domestic Judgment: 10, Foreign Judgment: 10
BAD CHECK LAWS (CIVIL PENALTY)
After 30 day written demand (certified or registered), twice check amount.
Attorney fees & court costs
GENERAL GARNISHMENT EXEMPTIONS
75% disposable earnings per work week, but not less than 30 x fed. min. hourly wage.
COLLECTION AGENCY BOND & LICENSE
Bond: Yes - $10,000
License: Yes
Fee:

All materials contained here-in are the property of the R.Sauger Company under US Copyright TX0005895316/203-12-16 or otherwise referred to as being available under the US Freedom of Information Act.

$200 Initial
$200 Investigation
$200 Renewal
$100 Branch
$100 Branch Renewal
114

....

MAINE
INTEREST RATE
Legal: 8%
Post Judgment: 15% annual (less than $30,000) T-Bill rate over $30,000
STATUTE OF LIMITATIONS (IN YEARS)
Open Acct.: 6,Written Contract: 6 + 20 (with attestment)
Domestic Judgment: 20, Foreign Judgment: 20
BAD CHECK LAWS (CIVIL PENALTY)
Amount due, court costs, service costs & collection costs
GENERAL GARNISHMENT EXEMPTIONS
You may garnish 25% of disposable income or 40 times the federal minimum wages per week (whichever is less) After judgment only.
COLLECTION AGENCY BOND & LICENSE
Bond: $25,000 to $50,000
License: Yes
Fee: $400 Yearly
Exemption for out-of-state collectors:
Contact state authority. Licensing authority is allowing some exemptions to outof-state agencies that collect for non-resident creditors and are not soliciting.

MARYLAND
INTEREST RATE
Legal: 6%
Judgment: 10% or contractual
STATUTE OF LIMITATIONS (IN YEARS)
Open Acct.: 3, UCC: 4, Specialty: 12 (contract under seal) ,Written Contract: 3
Domestic Judgment: 12, Foreign Judgment: 12
BAD CHECK LAWS (CIVIL PENALTY)
After 30 day written notice, amount due,
$25 fee, twice check amount up to $1000 (At the discretion of the court); Applies to COD sales only.
GENERAL GARNISHMENT EXEMPTIONS
Greater of 75% or amount = to $145 x no. of wks. in which wages due were earned; except in Caroline, Worchester, Kent & Queen Anne's Counties, see federal law. Exemption is up to $3,000 in cash and/or property for non-wage property exemption.
COLLECTION AGENCY BOND & LICENSE
Bond: $5000
License: Yes
Fee: $200 each office

All materials contained here-in are the property of the R.Sauger Company under US Copyright TX0005895316/203-12-16 or otherwise referred to as being available under the US Freedom of Information Act.

115
MASSACHUSETTS
INTEREST RATE
Legal: 6%
Judgment: 12%
Contract: 12%
STATUTE OF LIMITATIONS (IN YEARS)
Open Acct. other than Sales: 6, Contract: 6, Sales (UCC) Contract: 4
Domestic Judgment: 20 (presumed satisfied after 20 years), Foreign Judgment: 20, Contracts Under Seal: 20
BAD CHECK LAWS (CIVIL PENALTY)
Amount due, costs of suit, protest fees Additional damages $100 - $500 can be assessed.
GENERAL GARNISHMENT EXEMPTIONS $125 week
COLLECTION AGENCY BOND & LICENSE
Bond: $10,000 - $25,000
License: Yes
Fee: Determined by commissioner

MICHIGAN
INTEREST RATE
Legal: 5%
Judgment: 7.162 changes semi-annually
Usury limit 25%
STATUTE OF LIMITATIONS (IN YEARS)
Open Acct.: 6, Written Contract: 6, Sales (UCC) Contract: 4, Domestic Judgment: 10 renewable, Foreign Judgment: 10
BAD CHECK LAWS (CIVIL PENALTY)
Twice the amount of check-not to exceed $500. Retail Claims - Notice Requirements.
GENERAL GARNISHMENT EXEMPTIONS See federal law.
COLLECTION AGENCY BOND & LICENSE (RETAIL ONLY)
Bond: $5,000 - $50,000
License: Yes
Fee: $150 - Investigation $225 - Initial $125 - Annually
Exemption for out-of-state collectors:
Out-of-state collector are exempt if
[1] collecting by interstate means; and
[2] have no clients in the state of Michigan.

MINNESOTA
INTEREST RATE
Legal: 6%
Judgment: 5% (Changes Yearly)
Business or Agricultural Loan: 4.5% over federal discount rate
STATUTE OF LIMITATIONS (IN YEARS)
Goods Sold & Delivered (UCC): 4, Open Acct.: 6, Written Contract: 6,

All materials contained here-in are the property of the R.Sauger Company under US Copyright TX0005895316/203-12-16 or otherwise referred to as being available under the US Freedom of Information Act.

Transportation Service: 3
Domestic Judgment: 10, Foreign Judgment: 10
BAD CHECK LAWS (CIVIL PENALTY)
$100 or up to 100% of the value of the check, whichever is greater, plus interest at the rate payable on judgments on the face amount of check, plus reasonable attorney fees if aggregate amount of checks within 6 month period is over $1250.
GENERAL GARNISHMENT EXEMPTIONS
Greater of 75% or amount = to 40 x fed. min. hourly wage
COLLECTION AGENCY BOND & LICENSE
Bond: $5,000 to $20,000
License: Yes
Fee: $1,000 - Initial $400 - Annual $10 - Per Collector

MISSISSIPPI
INTEREST RATE
Legal: 8%
Judgment: amount in contract if no contract amount court decides
STATUTE OF LIMITATIONS (IN YEARS) Open
Acct.: 3, Written Contract: 3, UCC: 4
Domestic Judgment: 7, Foreign Judgment: 7 (3 if resident)
BAD CHECK LAWS (CIVIL PENALTY)
On checks up to and including $25.00, additional damages would be 100% of check amount. On checks from $25.01 to $200.00, additional damages would be 50% of check amount but not less than $25.00. On checks over $200.00 additional damages would be 25% of check amount.
GENERAL GARNISHMENT EXEMPTIONS See federal law.
COLLECTION AGENCY BOND & LICENSE Bond: No License: City-Business
Fee: $15-$50

MISSOURI
INTEREST RATE
Legal: 9%
Judgment: 9%
STATUTE OF LIMITATIONS (IN YEARS)
Sale of Goods: 4, Open Acct.: 5, Written Contract: 10
Domestic Judgment: 10 (Revived every 3 years), Foreign Judgment: 10 (Revived every 3 years)
BAD CHECK LAWS (CIVIL PENALTY)
Three times face amount owed or $100 whichever is greater not to exceed $500 (exclusive of attorney fees)
GENERAL GARNISHMENT EXEMPTIONS
See federal law; exempt 90% of week's net pay, head of household, single person w/o depend. = 75%
COLLECTION AGENCY BOND & LICENSE Bond: No License: No Fee: No

---

MONTANA
INTEREST RATE
Legal: 10%

Judgment: 10%
A binding written agreement may provide for interest of 15% or 6% above prime
STATUTE OF LIMITATIONS (IN YEARS)
Open Acct.: 5
Written Contract: 8
Domestic Judgment: 6 (over $5000) Renewable
Foreign Judgment: 6 Renewable
BAD CHECK LAWS (CIVIL PENALTY)
$100 minimum or 3 times face value up to $500
GENERAL GARNISHMENT EXEMPTIONS
See federal law.
COLLECTION AGENCY BOND & LICENSE
Bond: No
License: No
Fee: No
Caveats:
Foreign corporations should register with MT Sec. of State prior to any suit in MT Courts or risk dismissal.
Attorney fees only if provided by a signed written agreement.

NEBRASKA
INTEREST RATE
Legal: 12% per written instrument or contract rate
Judgment: 1% above bond equivalent yield as published by U.S. Treasury
STATUTE OF LIMITATIONS (IN YEARS)
Open Acct.: 4, Written Contract: 5
Domestic Judgment: 5 renewable every 5, Foreign Judgment: 5 non-renewable
BAD CHECK LAWS (CIVIL PENALTY)
Amount due, costs, protest fees
GENERAL GARNISHMENT EXEMPTIONS
Greater of 75% disposable earnings (85% if head of household), or 30 x fed. minimum hourly wage.
COLLECTION AGENCY BOND & LICENSE
Bond: Based on Lic. Solic. Less Than 5 = 5,000, 5-15=$10,000, 16-Up=$15,000
License: Yes
Fee: (not to exceed)
$250 - Investigation $200 - Original $100 - Renewal $50 - Investigation Branch Office $35 - Original Branch Office
Exemption for out-of-state collectors:
Out-of-state collectors are exempt IF
[1] communicating by interstate means (phone, fax, mail); and
[2] are "regulated" by the laws of another state.

NEVADA
INTEREST RATE
Legal: 2% Over Prime
Judgment: 2% Over Prime

All materials contained here-in are the property of the R.Sauger Company under US Copyright TX0005895316/203-12-16 or otherwise referred to as being available under the US Freedom of Information Act.

STATUTE OF LIMITATIONS (IN YEARS)
Open Account: 3, Open Acct-For Goods: 4, Written Contract: 6,Lease: 4
Domestic Judgment: 6, Foreign Judgment: 6
BAD CHECK LAWS (CIVIL PENALTY)
Amount due, protest fees three times check amount not more than $500, or less than $100
GENERAL GARNISHMENT EXEMPTIONS
Garnish only. 25% of Disposable earnings for each week or 30 times federal minimum hourly wage (whichever is less)
COLLECTION AGENCY BOND & LICENSE
Bond: $25,000 to $50,000
License: Yes
Fee: $250 - App. Survey $300 - Original $200 - Renewal
Exemption for out-of-state collectors:
Out-of-state collectors are exempt IF
[1] collecting by interstate means (phone, fax, mail); and
[2] collecting for an out-of-state client.

NEW HAMPSHIRE
INTEREST RATE
Judgment: 7.6%
STATUTE OF LIMITATIONS (IN YEARS)
Open Acct.: 3, For Goods: 4, Written Contract: 3, Written Contract/Negotiable Instrument:6, For Goods: 4
Domestic Judgment: 20,Foreign Judgment: 20
BAD CHECK LAWS (CIVIL PENALTY)
Amount due, interest, court costs, reasonable costs of collection & $10 per day (max. $50)
GENERAL GARNISHMENT EXEMPTIONS
50 x fed. min. hourly wage - All future wages are exempt so that the court cannot issue an ongoing order.
COLLECTION AGENCY BOND & LICENSE
Bond: No License: No Fee: No

NEW JERSEY
INTEREST RATE
Legal: 6%
Judgment: No Statutory Provision
STATUTE OF LIMITATIONS (IN YEARS)
Open Acct.: 3, Sale of Goods: 4, Written Contract: 6, Domestic Judgment: 20, Foreign Judgment: 20
BAD CHECK LAWS (CIVIL PENALTY) N/A
GENERAL GARNISHMENT EXEMPTIONS
$142.50 wk. min. 10% of gross earnings $142.50 & Over
COLLECTION AGENCY BOND & LICENSE
Bond: $5000 Surety License: No Fee: No

All materials contained here-in are the property of the R.Sauger Company under US Copyright TX0005895316/203-12-16 or otherwise referred to as being available under the US Freedom of Information Act.

NEW MEXICO
INTEREST RATE
Judgment: 8.75% (in the absence of a written contract)
STATUTE OF LIMITATIONS (IN YEARS)
Open Acct.: 4, Written Contract: 6, Domestic Judgment: 14, Foreign Judgment: 14
BAD CHECK LAWS (CIVIL PENALTY)
Amount due, triple damages up to $500 per check. Complex requirements need to be met.
GENERAL GARNISHMENT EXEMPTIONS
Greater of 75% or amount each wk. = to 40 x fed. min. hourly wage
COLLECTION AGENCY BOND & LICENSE
Bond: $5,000 minimum - based on volume License: Yes Fee: $500 - original collection agency or branch $300 - renewal collection agency or branch $100 - examination fee for manager's license $50 - manager renewal
Exemption for out-of-state collectors:
Out-of-state agency is exempt IF
[1] collecting by interstate means (phone, fax, mail); and
[2] debt was incurred outside the state of New Mexico.

NEW YORK
INTEREST RATE
Legal: 16%
Judgment: 9%
STATUTE OF LIMITATIONS (IN YEARS)
Open Acct.: 6, Written Contract: 6
Domestic Judgment: 20 (10 yr. renewable lien), Foreign Judgment: 20 (10 yr. renewable lien)
BAD CHECK LAWS (CIVIL PENALTY)
Face value of check plus two times check amount up to a maximum of $400 on NSF or $750 on "no account" (Demand prescribed by law). GEN.OB.1.1-104
GENERAL GARNISHMENT EXEMPTIONS
90% of earnings, except 1st $127.50 wk. wholly exempt.
COLLECTION AGENCY BOND & LICENSE
Bond: No
License: No
Fee: No
Buffalo: $5,000 Bond - $50 fee
NYC: License - $150 - 2 yr. fee

NORTH CAROLINA
INTEREST RATE
Legal: 8%
Judgment: 8%
STATUTE OF LIMITATIONS (IN YEARS)
Open Acct.: 3, Sale of Goods: 4, Written Contract: 3,
Domestic Judgment: 10, Foreign Judgment: 10

All materials contained here-in are the property of the R.Sauger Company under US Copyright TX0005895316/203-12-16 or otherwise referred to as being available under the US Freedom of Information Act.

BAD CHECK LAWS (CIVIL PENALTY)
30 day written demand lesser of $500 or 3x check amount, but not less than $100.
GENERAL GARNISHMENT EXEMPTIONS
100% of last 60 days' earnings for family support. Garnishment only by political subdivisions for taxes, ambulance fees, etc.
COLLECTION AGENCY BOND & LICENSE
Bond: $5,000 to $50,000 License: Yes Fee: $500
Exemption for out-of-state collectors:
Contact state authorities. Unofficially, licensing authorities may allow out-of-state agencies to bypass requirements if they do not solicit in state and/or work for instate clients.

NORTH DAKOTA
INTEREST RATE
Legal: 6%
Judgment: 12%
STATUTE OF LIMITATIONS (IN YEARS)
Open Acct. for services: 6, Sale of Goods: 4, Written Contract: 6
Domestic Judgment: 10 renewable, Foreign Judgment: 10 renewable
BAD CHECK LAWS (CIVIL PENALTY)
Amount due, collection fees of $20, and $100 or 3x check whichever is less.
GENERAL GARNISHMENT EXEMPTIONS
Greater of 75% or amount each wk. = to 40 x fed. min. hourly wage. Plus $20.00 each household dependent.
COLLECTION AGENCY BOND & LICENSE
Bond: $20,000 License: Yes Fee: $200
Exemption for out-of-state collectors:
Out-of-state collectors may be exempt IF
[1] collecting only;
[2] their office is located in a state that has a reciprocal law; and
[3] the state has "enacted similar legislation".

OHIO
INTEREST RATE
Legal: 10%
Judgment: 10%
STATUTE OF LIMITATIONS (IN YEARS)
Open Acct.: 4, Installment Sales Contract (UCC2-725) 6 ,Written Contract: 15
Domestic Judgment: 21 renew every 5, Foreign Judgment: 21 renew every 5
BAD CHECK LAWS (CIVIL PENALTY)
The greater of $200 or three times the amount of check and attorney fees (no maximum)
GENERAL GARNISHMENT EXEMPTIONS See federal law. Garnishment limited to once a month per employee.
COLLECTION AGENCY BOND & LICENSE
Bond: No License: No Fee: No

All materials contained here-in are the property of the R.Sauger Company under US Copyright TX0005895316/203-12-16 or otherwise referred to as being available under the US Freedom of Information Act.

OKLAHOMA
Exempted From TILA-Use Ok. Consumer Credit Statutes
INTEREST RATE
Legal: 6%
Judgment: 4% over U.S. Treasury Bill Rate of previous year. (1996 = 9.55% 1997 = 9.15%)
STATUTE OF LIMITATIONS (IN YEARS)
Oral and Open: 3 (note special arguments), Written Contract 5, Domestic Judgment: 5 renewable, Foreign Judgment: 3
BAD CHECK LAWS (CIVIL PENALTY) N/A
GENERAL GARNISHMENT EXEMPTIONS
State law: 75% of earnings exempted, more if hardship established. All federal exemptions apply.
COLLECTION AGENCY BOND & LICENSE
Bond: No License: No Fee: No

OREGON
INTEREST RATE
Statutory + Judgment: 9% simple interest per annum (Unless specified by contract)
STATUTE OF LIMITATIONS (IN YEARS)
Open Acct.: 6, Sale of Goods: 6 (4 yrs UCC Transaction), Written Contract: 6
Domestic Judgment: 10 - Renewable at 10, Foreign Judgment: 10
BAD CHECK LAWS (CIVIL PENALTY)
Can recover reasonable attorney fees & statutory damages of three times the amount of the NSF check plus$500 if demand letter is sent to debtor 30 days before suit is filed.
GENERAL GARNISHMENT EXEMPTIONS
75% of disposable earnings or 40 x fed. min. hourly wage.
COLLECTION AGENCY BOND & LICENSE
Bond: No License: Registration only Fee: Established by director
Exemption for out-of-state collectors:
Contact state authorities. Out-of-state agencies may be exempt IF
[1] collecting for out-of-state client;
[2] the debt was incurred by an Oregonian outside the state; and
[3] the state where the collection agency is headquartered has a registration program comparable to Oregon's law.

PENNSYLVANIA
INTEREST RATE
Legal: 6%
Judgment: 6%
STATUTE OF LIMITATIONS (IN YEARS)
Open Acct.: 4, Written Contract: 4,
Domestic Judgment: 5 (writ of revival within 5 yrs.), Foreign Judgment: 4,-Lien against real estate: 5 yrs. -Personal property Ex: 20 yrs.
BAD CHECK LAWS (CIVIL PENALTY)

All materials contained here-in are the property of the R.Sauger Company under US Copyright TX0005895316/203-12-16 or otherwise referred to as being available under the US Freedom of Information Act.

After demand and judgment triple damages in amount equal to $1 00 or 3 times the check amount whichever is greater up to $500.
GENERAL GARNISHMENT EXEMPTIONS
123
100%of wages, certain pensions, retirement accounts & Keogh plan under certain circumstances, and $300.
COLLECTION AGENCY BOND & LICENSE
Bond: No License: No Fee: No

RHODE ISLAND
INTEREST RATE
Legal: 12%
Judgment: 12%
STATUTE OF LIMITATIONS (IN YEARS)
Open Acct.: 3, Written Contract: 5, Contract Under Seal:10
Domestic Judgment: 20, Foreign Judgment: 20
BAD CHECK LAWS (CIVIL PENALTY)
Amount of check, $25 fee & treble damage up to $1000
GENERAL GARNISHMENT EXEMPTIONS
See federal law.
COLLECTION AGENCY BOND & LICENSE
Bond: No
License: No
Fee: No

SOUTH CAROLINA
INTEREST RATE
Legal: 8.75%
Judgment: 14%
STATUTE OF LIMITATIONS (IN YEARS)
Open Acct.: 3, Written Contract: 3,
Domestic Judgment: 10, Foreign Judgment: 10
BAD CHECK LAWS (CIVIL PENALTY)
Reasonable court costs amount of check& damages up to $500 or 3x check amount whichever is smaller
GENERAL GARNISHMENT EXEMPTIONS
100%
COLLECTION AGENCY BOND & LICENSE
Bond: No License: Yes - all business Fee: No
Exemption for out-of-state collectors:
License required for in-state agency only.

SOUTH DAKOTA
INTEREST RATE
Legal: 12%
Judgment: 10%
STATUTE OF LIMITATIONS (IN YEARS)

Open Acct.: 6, Sale of Goods: 4, Written Contract: 6
Domestic Judgment: 20, Foreign Judgment: 10
BAD CHECK LAWS (CIVIL PENALTY) N/A
GENERAL GARNISHMENT EXEMPTIONS
20% of the individuals disposable earnings for a 60 day period
COLLECTION AGENCY BOND & LICENSE
Bond: No License: No Fee: No

TENNESSEE
INTEREST RATE
Legal: 10%
Judgment: 10% (or contract rate) (varies with type of transaction)
STATUTE OF LIMITATIONS (IN YEARS)
Open Acct.: 3, Written Contract: 6
Domestic Judgment: 10, Foreign Judgment: 10
BAD CHECK LAWS (CIVIL PENALTY)
Treble damages up to $500 + 10% interest & reasonable service charges, Atty.'s fees, & court costs.
GENERAL GARNISHMENT EXEMPTIONS
See federal law. Add $2.50 per wk. for dependent child under 16.
COLLECTION AGENCY BOND & LICENSE
Bond: $15,000 1-4 employee $20,000 5-9 employee $25,000 10 or more
License: Yes Fee: $600 - Original $350 - Renewal $25 - Each Solicitor
Exemption for out-of-state collectors:
Contact state licensing authority. Out-of-state agencies MAY be exempt if they
[1] maintain office in another state;
[2] resides in a state that provides reciprocity; and
[3] comply with provisions of licensing.

TEXAS
INTEREST RATE*
Legal: 6% with agreement can charge up to 18%. w/o agreement - statutory interest of 6% begins to run 30th day after becoming due
Judgment: 10%
STATUTE OF LIMITATIONS (IN YEARS)
Open Acct.: 4, Written Contract: 4
Domestic Judgment: 10 (Renewable), Foreign Judgment: 10 (Renewable)
BAD CHECK LAWS (CIVIL PENALTY) N/A
GENERAL GARNISHMENT EXEMPTIONS
100% of Wages
COLLECTION AGENCY BOND & LICENSE
Bond: Yes License: No Fee: No
Always consult counsel to charge interest - Texas has very onerous usury laws & penalties.

UTAH
INTEREST RATE

All materials contained here-in are the property of the R.Sauger Company under US Copyright TX0005895316/203-12-16 or otherwise referred to as being available under the US Freedom of Information Act.

Legal: 7.35%
Judgment: Contract rate or Federal Judgment Rate
STATUTE OF LIMITATIONS (IN YEARS)
Open Acct.: 4, Written Contract: 6
Domestic Judgment: 8, Foreign Judgment: 8
BAD CHECK LAWS (CIVIL PENALTY)
Certified statutory bad check notice must be sent. Amount due, interest, court costs, reasonable attorney's fees, plus $15 bad check fee.
GENERAL GARNISHMENT EXEMPTIONS
$142.50 of disposable earnings for wages paid weekly.
COLLECTION AGENCY BOND & LICENSE
Bond: $10,000
License: Yes
Fee: Varies by City and County.

VERMONT
INTEREST RATE
Legal: 12%
Judgment: 12%
STATUTE OF LIMITATIONS (IN YEARS) Open Acct.: 3
to enforce an obligation, duty, or right arising under this article and not governed by this section must be commenced within three years after the [cause of action] accrues. (Added 1993, No. 158 (Adj. Sess.), § 12, eff. Jan. 1, 1995.)
Written Contract: 6
Domestic Judgment: 8
Foreign Judgment: 8
BAD CHECK LAWS (CIVIL PENALTY)
Court costs, amount of check, attorney's fees, damage of $50. (Notices required)
GENERAL GARNISHMENT EXEMPTIONS
75% of earning above minimum wage or what is necessary to live.
COLLECTION AGENCY BOND & LICENSE
Bond: No License: No Fee: No

VIRGINIA
INTEREST RATE
Legal: 8%
Judgment: 9% or contract rate whichever is higher
STATUTE OF LIMITATIONS (IN YEARS)
Open Acct.: 3 Last charge or payment, Sales of goods 4 years, Written Contract: 5
Domestic Judgment: 20, Foreign Judgment: 10
BAD CHECK LAWS (CIVIL PENALTY)
Lesser of $250 or three times check amount
GENERAL GARNISHMENT EXEMPTIONS
See federal law
COLLECTION AGENCY BOND & LICENSE
Bond:$5000 License: Depends on Locality Fee: No

All materials contained here-in are the property of the R.Sauger Company under US Copyright TX0005895316/203-12-16 or otherwise referred to as being available under the US Freedom of Information Act.

WASHINGTON
INTEREST RATE
Legal: 12%
Judgment: 12%
STATUTE OF LIMITATIONS (IN YEARS)
Open Acct.: 3, Written Contract: 6,
Domestic Judgment: 10, Foreign Judgment: 10
BAD CHECK LAWS (CIVIL PENALTY)
Lesser of check amount or 12% interest, collection costs up to $40. If taken to court, reasonable attorney's fees, 3 x value, or up to $300. Now have 6 years to enforce a bad check.
GENERAL GARNISHMENT EXEMPTIONS
Greater of 75% or $64 wk. (40 x state min. hourly wage).
COLLECTION AGENCY BOND & LICENSE
Bond: $6000 general, $4000 specialty
License: Yes
Fee: $100 - Investigation $100 - Original $100 - Renewable $50 - Branch Office
Exemption for out-of-state collectors: Contact state authorities. Out-of-state agencies MAY qualify for lesser licensing fees. Out-of-state collectors are no longer required to have resident office and in-state trust accounts if they don't have in-state client. Bond is not required if held in home state.

WEST VIRGINIA
INTEREST RATE
Legal: 6%
Judgment: 10%
STATUTE OF LIMITATIONS (IN YEARS)
Open Acct.: 5, Written Contract: 10
Domestic Judgment: 10, Foreign Judgment: 10
BAD CHECK LAWS (CIVIL PENALTY)
Amount due, service charge up to $10. If check is under $500.00 = misdemeanor. Over $500.00 = felony.
GENERAL GARNISHMENT EXEMPTIONS
See West Va code 38-5A-3-Employees withhold 20% of disposable income or 30x the minimum hourly rate, whichever is less. Other exemptions apply.
COLLECTION AGENCY BOND & LICENSE
Bond: $5,000 License: Yes - Franchise Reg. Cert. Fee: $15 Annual
Exemption for out-of-state collectors: Contact state authorities. Some out-of-state agencies MAY be exempt if they are only collecting for out-of-state clients.

WISCONSIN
INTEREST RATE
Legal: 5%
Judgment: 12%
STATUTE OF LIMITATIONS (IN YEARS)
Open Acct.: 6, Written Contract: 6

All materials contained here-in are the property of the R.Sauger Company under US Copyright TX0005895316/203-12-16 or otherwise referred to as being available under the US Freedom of Information Act.

Domestic Judgment: 20, Foreign Judgment: 20
BAD CHECK LAWS (CIVIL PENALTY)
Amount of check plus actual damages + exemplary damages up to three times value of check. Limited to $300.
GENERAL GARNISHMENT EXEMPTIONS
80% of net pay.
COLLECTION AGENCY BOND & LICENSE
Bond: $15,000 min. License: Yes Fee: $1000 - Investigation $200 - Annual
Exemption for out-of-state collectors:
Out-of-state agencies do not need to be licensed if
[1] collecting by interstate means (phone, fax, mail); and
[2] collecting for an out-of-state client.

WYOMING
INTEREST RATE
Legal: 7%
Judgment: contract rate or 10% judgment rate
STATUTE OF LIMITATIONS (IN YEARS)
Open Acct.: 8, Written Contract: 10
Domestic Judgment: 5, Foreign Judgment: 5
BAD CHECK LAWS (CIVIL PENALTY)
Double the face amount plus damages equal to collection cost and reasonable attorney fees.
GENERAL GARNISHMENT EXEMPTIONS
See Federal law for consumer credit sale, lease or loan. Up to 65% for child support arrearage.
COLLECTION AGENCY BOND & LICENSE
Bond: $10,000 License: Yes Fee: $200 - Original $100 - Renewal $100 - Branch
Exemption for out-of-state collectors:
Out-of-state agencies MAY bypass licensing if they are not
[1] soliciting clients in Wyoming; or
[2] collecting for Wyoming creditors.

All materials contained here-in are the property of the R.Sauger Company under US Copyright TX0005895316/203-12-16 or otherwise referred to as being available under the US Freedom of Information Act.

Made in the USA
Columbia, SC
06 November 2023